SPECIAL EDUCATION:

A Parent's Guide for a Child's Success

Michael T. Bailey

Foreword by Curt Decker

PublishAmerica
Baltimore

At the specific preference of the author, PublishAmerica allowed this work to remain exactly as the author intended, verbatim, without editorial input.

ISBN: 1-4241-2795-5
PUBLISHED BY PUBLISHAMERICA, LLLP
www.publishamerica.com
Baltimore

Printed in the United States of America

DEDICATION

For my beautiful daughters,

Eleanor Sumner Bailey

and

Taylor Sumner Bailey,

and to the memory of

Justin Dart, Jr.,

this dream of an inclusive, happy and

brave life is dedicated.

ACKNOWLEDGMENTS

No one has supported efforts to make Eleanor's education a success more than her loving grandparents, Robert and Kathryn Bailey and John and Retha Schuder. Thank you. It could not be done without you. Special thanks to Jonna Schuder for being such a wonderful mother to our daughters, and such a good friend, advisor and confidant to me.

There are many people involved in disability rights who have inspired and emboldened me. Special thanks to the late Eldridge Cleaver for his many kindnesses. Also Bob Kafka, Stephanie Thomas, Marsha Katz, Bob Liston and Kyle Glozier from ADAPT. Additionally, Joelle Brouner, Diane Coleman, Tia Nelis, Nancy Ward, Nancy Weiss, Bud Thoune, Steve Drake, Marsha Forest, Jack Pierpoint, Dan Wilkins, Judith Snow and Eric Treat. Thanks for the courage and leadership.

Basil McDermott, Larry Olstad and Frank Lundburg for years and years of friendship. Lucy Gwin of Kansas for proving that truth can still be told.

Janine Bertram Kemp for her selfless friendship, encouragement and courage. Yoshiko Dart for keeping the dream alive. Curt Decker, Kathy McGinley and Janna Starr for proving that good people can be effective in Washington, DC. As they demonstrate everyday, selling out is optional.

In Germany, my dear Susanne Göbel. In Hawaii, Steve Brown and the Center for the Study of Disability Culture have always given freely. Steve Gold for being the best lawyer in the world. Tom Olin for being the best photographer.

Steadfast friends have made suggestions and offered needed support. Thanks to Jeanne Farr, Tim Kral, Ron Taylor, Kathy Favali, Jan Campbell and Bob Joondeph. My two dear pals, Maxine Kilcrease and Charlotte Duncan for keeping me intellectually honest and on track. Harriett McBryde Johnson for being herself.

Thanks to my special education moms who "get it." Joan Guthrie-Medlen, Laura Soyster, Kathleen Priest, Arlene Marshall, Elaine Piper-Vardas, Evelyn Lowry, Sonya Fischer and Angela Jarvis-Holland. You guys deserve all good things.

Finally, special thanks to Carolyn Lieberg for believing in this project, encouraging me, and for her hours of editing and proofreading. Thanks for everything my dear.

Table of Contents

Chapter 3 ~School-Age Children

The Heart and Soul of Services   75

Part I

Part II

Part III

Part IV

Chapter 4 ~Other IDEA Services

Chapter 5 ~Advocacy and Problem Solving

Chapter 6 ~Inclusion

Chapter 7 ~Conflict Resolution

Chapter 8 ~The Future of Special Education

Glossary

Appendix

FOREWORD

Curtis Decker, JD
Executive Director
National Disability Rights Network

In 1975, when P.L. 94-142 (later to become IDEA and now IDEIA) was passed, a milestone was reached in the disability civil rights movement. This legislation was a result of lawsuits brought by frustrated and angry parents who demanded that their children be educated by the public school system and not relegated to large, congregate, out-of-the-way facilities – so called "training schools." This new law was the forerunner of principles that have directed the disability movement for the last thirty years. IDEA embodies the concepts of the disability movement – choice, independence, least restrictive environment and inclusion.

Additionally, the new law envisioned parental control over direction in the education of their children and established a strong system of due process protections that would force an entrenched system to open itself up to children with disabilities who had experienced education discrimination for decades. If this new law were implemented appropriately, every child with a disability would be able to reach his or her full potential within the nation's public education system.

Over the last thirty years, millions of children with a wide range of disabilities have received an education alongside their non-disabled peers. There are wonderful success stories of children who would have been shunted off to special schools or institutions if it were not for the protections of IDEA. In fact, the single major reason that only a small number of young children and teenagers remain in large congregate public institutions throughout the country (Breedlove, Decker, Lakin) is the entitlement to an inclusive education mandated by IDEA.

These accomplishments, however, were not achieved without a long and difficult struggle by parents and their allies. Parents had to resort to aggressive advocacy including administrative and legal action, to force the system to respond to their needs.

Moreover, the wonderful concepts and great promise associated with the enactment of P.L. 94-142 have not materialized for all children and their parents – at least not to the extent that parents, advocates, and many educators and policymakers had so hopefully envisioned. A myriad of barriers have sprung up to keep many children from receiving the education to which they are entitled. Those barriers include recalcitrant administrators, over-worked and undertrained teachers, inadequate or non-existent assessments, inadequate specialists, a devastating lack of resources and overt discrimination against children with disabilities. This pattern of discrimination not only has denied access to education but at times also has resulted in serious physical and mental harm.

Despite the fact that the concepts in IDEIA are sound and well proven, the regular education system has worked effectively to undercut the protections and guarantees of the law.

It has not helped the full implementation of IDEIA that Congress has failed to live up to its original promise of a federal/state partnership. When the law was first enacted, the major sponsors promised a federal share of resources equal to 40% of the cost of implementing this mandate. Over the last decades, the federal participation has hovered at only 6% and climbed recently to just 10% of the total cost of special education. Despite efforts to "fully fund" IDEA, the money has not materialized, thereby placing a severe burden on states and local education agencies and adding to the backlash and resistance to fully adhere to the requirements that parents have come to expect.

Additionally, there has generally been a dearth of resources for enforcement of IDEA. The Congress has funded the Parent Information Centers to train parents. The Protection and Advocacy systems have taken the lead in providing special education advocacy and are the largest enforcer of the Act but without specific resources to do so. The private bar has also been a resource to some limited extent. The Office of Civil Rights in the Department of Education has a less than impressive record in enforcing the act.

This means that the quest to achieve a free and appropriate education for their children falls on the shoulders of parents. Like it or not, parents of children with disabilities are going to need to advocate for themselves in most instances. Even if the parents receive some additional assistance, they will need to be informed and vigilant throughout the process.

I do not want to be completely negative. Despite all the problems that have been faced, there have been tremendous successes, and millions of children with disabilities have benefited from the mandates of this amazing law. Several generations of children have grown up with their peers with disabilities. People with disabilities now are accepted as members of our communities where they live, work, and play.

Michael Bailey's book is a wonderful primer for parents who must navigate this difficult, fast-changing and intimidating system. Even with assistance from professional advocacy organizations, parents need to be informed and prepared to do most of the work themselves. This is why this book is so important.

Michael has written with a combination of concrete information, effective strategies, and a realistic look at the many phases of the parenting and education process, sage advice, and humor. His own personal story as a parent of a wonderful daughter with a disability illustrates the many issues to be faced from birth through early childhood intervention programs to elementary and middle school and beyond. This book is essential reading for parents, their children, and even professionals who need to reeducate themselves about the reason IDEIA was enacted in the first place.

Washington, DC
February 2006

Introduction

Out of the sighs a love comes
At last, in hail and rain
Upon your held-out hand
Nearly summer, and the devil
Poem
Were that enough, enough to ease the pain

The Notebook Poems
Dylan Thomas

This is a book for parents like me. Parents of children with disabilities.

We know things.

Special education is one of the things we know. We know what the word "special" means. And we know what it means to experience primordial emotions.

Parents navigating the legal, regulatory, and human maze called special education know that there is more to it than knowing rules and procedures. We know that we, and we alone, are responsible for protecting our child while, at the same time, educating them. We know how it feels to see them isolated and singled out. We know what it is like to wonder what will happen to them when we are dead and they aren't.

What will happen?

All of us have a memory, of breathlessness and an electric-like spasm down the spine, when "they" uttered the words, "Your child has a disability."

"How is that possible?" "How could this happen to me?"

We bury our secret memory of the look on our own parents' faces when we emerged, ashen and shaking, from a delivery room or diagnosis, and said to them some unthinkable things about their grandchild.

Most of us had different friends before our child's birth. Our friends were, naturally, ever so kind. Friends brought the gifts. But we all have a secret memory of how they gently withdrew their own perfect children, as if disability were a communicable disease, as if they feared we couldn't stand to see children without disabilities. Those old friendships didn't die so much as they just faded away. These are the things we know.

We remember how we learned what it means to be a true stranger in a truly strange land.

A day came when I realized it wasn't about me or Eleanor's mom. It was about Eleanor. The moment came when I knew that this was the only life this little person will have. That day I imagined myself as her and wondered what my life would be like if I were she. What would it be like if I never got a moment's respite from the stigma of being different? That's an important memory. Using the moment of realization as a starting point, I, and all of us, can began to ponder what we can do to make this, our child's one and only life, the best it can be.

Some people have memories of secret rituals – a make-believe funeral for the expected child not born, a bitter afternoon of tearing down and destroying a nursery you had so lovingly prepared. We all have our secrets. No one but us knows them. And there is a reason.

When our children were born we didn't know there were so many social workers, clergy, busybodies, therapists, physicians, educators, and case managers. But they come to us with the inevitability of the changing seasons.

No matter what we may want to believe and what we sometimes say, we know there is a huge difference between "us" and "them." They all chose this work. They spent years learning their craft and learning how to deal with us. We meet them on very unfair and unfamiliar ground. We depend on them and, at the same time, we secretly resent them.

There are many things we learn. That there will always be officials and experts in our lives is one of them. Learning to work with them and benefit from their expertise is one skill that can't be compromised or minimized.

All of us have special professionals in our memory to whom we owe a never-to-be repaid debt for their kindness, patience, and insight. But another secret we have is the loathing memory of the ones who did not respect our child or us; the ones anxious to demonstrate their superiority and skill; the ones who tell us what to do; the ones who know it all; the ones with the condescending voices. We all share a secret memory of having our grief trivialized and sidelined by words like "denial." We remember those things.

There are many books on special education. Most of them are written for college students or professional practitioners. Some of them are written by academics or professional advocates. They all are important contributions. But there are few books written only for parents.

This is one such book. There is an enormous amount of information we must master in order to effectively advocate for our children.

Having a child with a disability is a lot like going to medical school, law school and wilderness survival camp, all at once.

This book will give you plenty of information about laws and regulations, meetings and personalities, strategies for success. But I have also written personal memories. They are not included because they are unique. They are here to remind you of your own stories. They are here to help you use your own memory as a powerful tool. You survived the trauma of having a child with a disability. You are a strong person. Learn to use your amazing strength to master one more thing required of you: Become an effective special education advocate.

This undertaking cannot be just labor and struggle. We need a sense of humor and we need to remember that this is about love. Disability uncovers a lot of hypocrisy. Bitterness will consume you if you let it. But the primitive, animal love parents have for children is a powerful tool. Keeping your child in the center of every picture will see you through some unimaginably terrible times. This struggle is about our children, and that is all it is about.

This book, too, is about learning not to be ashamed. It is about learning from other parents. It is about, more than anything, learning to believe in your child. It is about learning from them. And, it is about accepting them.

I organized this book in a way that gives information necessary to master the art of special education advocacy while giving equal attention to the unique experience of being a parent to a child with a disability. Our power comes not just with knowledge but also with the collective wisdom of our own experience, trauma, and growth, and the experiences of other parents.

Learning is not an experience that is easy. We get better at it and we learn to master most of it but some hurts and injuries are ours alone. We mostly keep them secret. But they are our most important source of strength.

…

I don't remember precisely when Little Foot, the adorable dinosaur from "Land Before Time" came into our lives. Both of our daughters fell in love with him, I know that. And before long we had not one film but five. We loved "Little Foot."

Christmas vacation for grade school age kids is an odd time. The week before Christmas is all excitement and expectation. The week after is a le down that leaves parents wondering how to fill the time. I came up with what I thought was a brilliant idea. We would sponsor a "Land Before Time" film festival!

I suggested this to the girls, who were very excited about using our home video camera, eating pizza, seeing their friends, and watching the films. Each of them invited five friends from school, and we waited for the day to come.

At the appointed time, cars began arriving and mothers and fathers dropped off their excited children. My girls were full of anticipation. I must admit, children that age look a lot alike to me. I had no idea which ones were invited by my daughter with a disability and which by her sister, Taylor.

As the children arrived, they went off happily to the television room, except for Eleanor, who stood on her short and sturdy legs in an easy chair in the front room window and looked sadly out into the empty street. I could see that she was near tears. "What's the matter sweetheart?" I asked her.

"But Daddy," she said," Where are my friends?"

None of the kids she invited came. None of their parents felt a child with a disability was important enough for an RSVP. The hurt on her face was a real lesson for me. The hurt in my heart is a secret that I keep.

21

...

Every parent who reads this book has had a moment like mine. A moment where we learn that we are on our own. Where we learn that other parents, no matter how well intended they may be, will never understand.

We all share that secret.

We can love and respect our professional colleagues, and we do, but we know some things they don't.

This book is about using the things we know in a way that we hope will help us make our children happy and independent human beings who are proud of themselves. Our children, we hope, will know the difference between what is true and right in this world and what is not.

We are not people who chose this life because we found it "interesting." We have no financial or professional stake in special education. We are just people whom, one day, had some reality dropped in our lap. We live with the reality, not because we chose it, but because we had no choice.

This is a book about facts and laws and regulations and customs and culture and acceptance and fear and joy and life. It is not idealized, sanitized, or romanticized.

It is about how we have learned to cope every day with stuff we never wanted to know. It is about optimism and spirit. It is about families. It is about fear. It is about becoming comfortable with fear and not letting it dictate how we live or raise our children. It is about overcoming big challenges. It is about life.

It is about all of us with secrets.

Chapter 1

SPECIAL EDUCATION

*"What I would like to see is people with
disabilities themselves actually feel that we are
fully entitled to be part of society."*

Stephanie Thomas

Things to Know
What is Special Education?
What is FAPE?
Who is a "Child with a Disability?"
Who Receives Special Education?
What is IDEA?
What is Section 504?
Section 504: What is a Major Life Activity?
Section 504: What is an Accommodation?
Spirituality
Attend trainings

Things to Know

The right of children with disabilities to a free and appropriate public education is the law in the United States. It has been for decades. But that right is still treated as if it were something new and revolutionary. Old prejudices die-hard. Facing down prejudice is the biggest hurdle families must overcome in order to advocate for their "special needs" child.

Special education is simply a logical extension of phenomena that began with the social reformist movement of the 19th Century. The creation of public schools, and the concept of a free public education for all, came from that reform agenda. Unfortunately, as is too often the case with disabilities, such things as giant institutions and separation from family and community can also be traced to the same historic period. Our children have had things done "for them" and they also have experienced the other side of good intentions, which is having things done "to them." If, as if often said, the road to hell is paved with good intentions, our kids have been in the cross hairs way too often.

The first rule of good advocacy is to make yourself stop believing that your child is "special." That makes people feel like they are guests in the real world. Guests with an invitation that is revocable at will. Our kids are not guests. They belong here. They have the right to expect an education and a life that will make them happy, independent, proud, and valued. Your attitude is the starting point for achieving those goals. Believe in your child's future and value. Start believing that today. Your belief is catching. Infect the world with it.

Who, precisely, would attend these new public schools were not so much defined as implicitly understood. A public education did not mean, in the mind of parents, educators or politicians, an equal education for Afro-American children. It certainly did not mean one for children with disabilities.

For most of the 20th Century children, with disabilities were simply out of sight and out of mind. Tens of thousands of them were separated from their families at birth and warehoused in giant state institutions called "training centers." Little if any training ever happened anywhere. The overwrought managers of these places were happy to simply get the children fed.

In 1954 that lack of clarity was changed drastically by the U.S. Supreme Court decision known as *Brown v. The Board of Education.* The Supreme Court explicitly ruled that an educational system presented as "separate but equal," was unconstitutional. From that point on American children have had the right to attend neighborhood schools without regard to race. *Brown* did not address the question of how to educate children with disabilities. What it did do was raise awareness of the possibilities. It was left, not to courts, but to parents to do something about the education of their children with disabilities.

Ideas such as education, recreation, and the trappings of normal living for kids with disabilities were simply not on the radar of awareness. "They belong with their own kind," was a mantra that made all sorts of abuse acceptable under the guise of care and charity.

Happily, most of those institutions closed as cultural thinking about disability changed. With more children than ever living at home with their families the question arose, "What to do with them?"

Since schools had no obligation to accept children with disabilities, parents began to band together to attempt to educate their children the best they could. Typically, a group of mothers would combine with a church basement for some kind of "activity center" that resembled, somewhat, a school. Paid staff, consultants, experts and curriculum, for kids with disabilities were still in the future.

But the experience of seeing children with disabilities benefit from community living raised the expectations of parents. The result was the founding of local, state, and national organizations that began to bring their collective power to bear on politicians.

The result was educational reform on an unprecedented scale. That reform culminated in the enactment of the Individuals with Disabilities Education Act. (IDEA). Although IDEA has been amended several times since its adoption, its underlying principles remain the same.

IDEA brought to all children with disabilities the federally guaranteed right to a free and appropriate public education (FAPE). The whole direction of this book will be to help families understand their legal rights and, of equal importance, give them the practical tools necessary to succeed as educational advocates for their children.

We will return again and again to the basic philosophical lynchpin of IDEA. Your child enjoys an enforceable right to a free and appropriate public education. That is the foundation. The rest is detail.

What Is Special Education?

Special education, in the minds of many, are those little yellow school buses that move around neighborhoods and take kids in wheelchairs to school. To others special education is something they cannot imagine having a personal stake in.

To way too many people, the idea of having a child with a disability and entanglement with special education is akin to their worst nightmare.

It is likely that you, the reader, were once one of those people. I know I was.

But for us the joys have outstripped the trauma. The more you know about your child, the possibility of a quality education and an adulthood of independence and self-direction, the more positive the picture will become. It is said that information is power. Let's start our empowerment by defining special education.

Federal law regards special education as instruction that is specifically designed to meet the unique needs of a child with a disability and is provided at no cost to parents.

Special education is simply specially designed curriculum to meet the unique educational needs of each child. It is a brilliant idea. It should be applied to all children and not just the ones with the labels that make them "eligible."

Special education services must be designed for one child at a time. It is helpful to imagine regular education as a "cookie-cutter" model where everyone is offered the same basic program. Special education is the opposite; it is handmade for each child, one at a time.

So far we know that our child with a disability has the right to a free and appropriate public education and the right to a plan of learning that is designed specifically to meet his or her educational needs. This is a simple concept. Try your best to keep it that way. This is about the right of one child at a time to go to school. That is all it's about.

Adults, naturally, have confused and complicated what should be easy and simple. There are laws and rules that you must know in order to succeed. The rest of this book will give them to you. They can seem impossibly confusing and contradictory. They can be discouraging. Stick to the basics. It's simple.

Your child has the right to a free and appropriate public education. They have the right to specially designed instruction. They have the right to receive their education in an environment that emphasizes their normalcy and not their differences.

Special education is designed to provide accommodations, modifications and specialized curriculum necessary to enable children with disabilities to access public education. It is fundamentally a civil rights law that is based on a long history of discrimination against, and the exclusion of, students with disabilities.

The captain of this great ship of learning is you, the parent. Your participation is the key to success. You have the right to direct it. But like any good captain, there are things you must know before you can steer the ship.

The first thing you need to know is that there are four federal laws that impact education and children with disabilities. The two most important, and the ones we will dwell on, are IDEA and Section 504 of the Rehabilitation Act. The others are The Americans with Disabilities Act and the law popularly referred to as "No Child Left Behind." The latter two we will work in here and there. What you need to know is IDEA and Section 504.

What Is FAPE?

FAPE is an acronym that stands for Free and Appropriate Public Education. "Free" means just what it says – each eligible child with a disability has the right to receive a public education at no cost to parents. "Appropriate" means specially designed curriculum developed to meet the educational needs of one child at a time. Your main job is to help identify and meaningfully implement what is appropriate for your child.

Remember a FAPE must be provided to each child with a disability according to the educational plan developed for that individual child. That plan is called an "Individual Education Program," or IEP, and is the cornerstone of service delivery. There are detailed discussions of IEP development throughout this book.

The challenge to parents and school personnel is that FAPE means something different for every child, because each child's "individual needs" are different.

That is why the law is called the INDIVIDUALS with Disabilities Education Act. If Congress had intended a "one-size-fits-all" law it would be called the Disabilities Education Act. Each child's needs must be considered individually and each child's educational program must be planned according to those individual needs.

Who Is a "Child with a Disability?"

To qualify for educational services under IDEA, or Section 504, the child must be a "child with a disability." In ordinary language we call that eligibility. This is discussed in detail elsewhere. For now it is enough to note that the process of evaluation for services must find that your child falls into some category of disability AND needs special education services.

Although categories vary slightly from state to state the basic parameters are:

Speech and Language impairments.

Hearing impairments (including deafness).

Mental retardation.

Visual impairments (including blindness).

Traumatic brain injury.

Specific learning disabilities. (These are conditions that impair the ability to listen, think, write, spell, read, do math, etc. They include, for example, such things as dyslexia and non-verbal learning disabilities.)

Orthopedic Impairments. (Including bone diseases, fractures, burns, cerebral palsy.)

Autism. (Commonly defined as a condition affecting communication and social interaction.) and

Other Health Impairments. (These include chronic or acute health problems such as asthma, leukemia, diabetes, epilepsy, etc.)

The child must have one of these conditions plus the need for special education services. A child's need for services is the deciding factor.

Who Receives Special Education?

Obviously all children with disabilities are entitled to receive services. The public's perception probably is one of kids with very severe disabilities. But most of the children in special education are diagnosed with conditions that are fairly minor on the disability continuum. The majority of children in special education will leave it when their disabling conditions change.

Although states vary somewhat, it is interesting to look at the eligibility criteria for my own state, Oregon. These are pretty typical from year to year and from state to state.

Disability	# of Students	% of Students
Specific Learning Disability	33,941	45.9%
Speech and Hearing	18,358	24.8%
Other health impaired	4,350	5.8%
Emotional Disturbance	4,344	5.8%
Mental Retardation	4,273	5.7%
Developmental Delay	3,279	4.4%
Autism	2,548	3.4%
Hearing/Deaf	1,038	1.4%
Orthopedic Impairment	1.031	1.4%
Vision/Blind	388	.53%
Brain Injury	309	.42%
Deaf and Blind	28	.04%

Politically it is important for you to note that the majority of these students have pretty minor needs and do not require expensive, life-long services. The right to a FAPE for your child is not impairing, in the least, the educational rights and opportunities of others.

What Is IDEA?

The federal education law specifically designed for children with disabilities is called the Individuals with Disabilities Education Act (IDEA). IDEA requires that all states receiving money from the federal government accept, along with the money, the obligation of providing a FAPE to every child with a disability. (Following adoption of the 2004 Amendments the law became officially known as the Individuals with Disabilities Education Improvement Act – IDEIA.)

If your child fits the eligibility criteria listed above, and needs services, those services will be provided under IDEA. There is ample information regarding details on IDEA in specific chapters of this book.

Keep in mind that if your child is eligible for services under IDEA they are also entitled to all the accommodations and benefits of Section 504.

But, what if your child needs special assistance in school but does require the level of service provided by IDEA? In other words, what if they need help but are not eligible under IDEA?

What Is Section 504?

Section 504 is a federal law which makes it illegal to discriminate against an otherwise qualified person because of disability. It is not an Education Law, but it applies to students with disabilities. Schools are required to take steps to give students with disabilities access to all programs and activities offered by the school!

Unlike IDEA, Section 504 does not require that a student with a disability have a detailed Individual Education Program (IEP). However, most states require a 504 plan to be in writing and most have adopted the same procedures as those used for IEPs. There are written procedures and remedies in your state for enforcing the requirements of a 504 plan. You can obtain details from your state department of education or, probably, the principal or special education director of your school.

Programs and activities covered by Section 504 may be either public or private, and include businesses, colleges, recreational facilities, health care, and housing as well as education. The law protects the right of a person with a disability to participate in programs or activities that are available to people without disabilities. This means making "accommodations" for the student's disability.

The accommodation is designed to assure participation in programs and activities that may not be accessible without the accommodation.

Your child is protected by Section 504 if they have a physical or mental impairment that substantially limits one or more major life activities; or if your child has a personal history of such impairment or is regarded as having such impairment.

A child with HIV or AIDS cannot be treated differently because of his or her diagnosis.

A student cannot be denied the opportunity to enroll in science class in high school because of a history of special education in elementary school.

Naturally this language is confusing. What does it mean?

Section 504:
What Is a "Major Life Activity?"

Section 504 is a more general law than IDEA. It covers more students and more types of activities and programs. The education rights of students under Section 504 are the same as IDEA and a "504 Plan," in most states, is simply written the same as an IEP.

Major life activities under Section 504 includes seeing, learning, doing manual tasks, self-care, hearing, breathing, walking, speaking and working.

Section 504:
What Is an "Accommodation?"

Accommodation means "help," "assistance," "support," or "adjustment." It can mean whatever you want it to mean if it assures participation in programs and activities.

For one student it may mean extra time on a test and for another, assistance with note taking. My daughter is pretty small. She is in high school and has lots of big textbooks. She cannot carry them, her computer, and all her other stuff, too, and from home. She has an accommodation of two sets of books, one at school and one at home.

Accommodation also means accessible. This means wheelchair ramps, special procedures for fire drills, and elevators. It can mean help getting seated for a school sporting event, dance, or play. For other students, accessible may mean alternative methods of communication, Braille or sign language, or specially designed computer programs.

IDEA, Section 504, and various state laws combine to guarantee a wide range of rights to individuals with disabilities. IDEA is a complex law. It is discussed in detail, as I have said.

Take this one step at a time. If you have read this far, you have learned the basics. To these basics, add your own confidence that you are the world's leading expert on your own child. The law provides you with the right to participate in every aspect of your child's education. It is a powerful right. Learn to use it effectively. The most important skill is a belief in yourself, your child, and your family.

You absolutely need not be a lawyer or a special education professional to do this well. When it comes to the services your child needs, it is up to you, in cooperation, perhaps, with trained professionals, to identify the needs. It is up to the school to provide the personnel in order to assure that the needs are met.

How to Use This book

If you have not done so take time to read the Table of Contents. Find what you need to know now. Learn that and don't worry about knowing everything at once.

Do not confuse what you read here with legal advice. For a specific fact situation in your community there is no substitute for advice from a local lawyer with advanced expertise in special education.

If your child is a toddler or infant, then put your energy into learning what an Individual Family Support Plan is. There is plenty of time later in life to worry about IEP meetings and Transition Plans.

There are web resources at the end of the book. Look at them and find the ones that help you. There are many good resources available on the web. Networking with other parents is of great importance. There are chat groups, blogs and support groups everywhere.

Having a child with a disability does not mean that you automatically become best friends with every other parent in our situation. It does mean that you will probably find that other parents are able to understand your fear and sense of unreality about some of this. It is important for you to remember that you are not the first person to go through this. Other parents' and their experiences are of great importance. You can learn from others. This is a hard area to do alone. There is too much riding on the outcome, too much pathos, and, potentially, too much conflict.

But your best weapon goes back to the quote at the beginning of this chapter. You must learn to really, in your heart-of-hearts, believe that you and your child belong to our society. You are not a guest. This is your life.

Neither Congress nor schools handed us IDEA or other laws. There was no day on which educators looked at their schools and noticed there were no children with disabilities and set out to include them. No, parents just like us thought up the rights we enjoy. They changed the world for the better. They gave to you the opportunity not only to have your child educated for free in a public school but they empowered you with the right to be a part of all decisions.

I know that special education advocacy is challenging, hard, hurtful, and complicated. Look at it as an opportunity, an opportunity you have only because parents just like you believed in themselves and their children enough to change the educational world.

Spirituality

Whatever it takes to get you through this is what you must do. For many people of faith there are answers to be found there. For others, meditation or exercise is equally helpful. This is the most personal thing you will experience. You don't have to be answerable to anyone for how you choose to deal with it.

But one common truth is that you are of no value to your child unless you are healthy physically and emotionally. If you are in a relationship, nurture it. Take time for you and your spouse or partner to get away.

Everyone handles this stress in a different way. I strongly believe in not making judgments about what other parents chose to do. But I don't think anyone is well served when I talk to mothers who let me know that their teenager with a disability has slept with or near them every single night of their life. You need a break and so does your child.

You have the right to a relationship. You have the right to good health and happiness. Even if you currently think that the needs of your child with a disability have taken over your life, you must stop and think again. Parents who do not take care of themselves and their needs will soon be of no use to anyone, their child included.

If you need a support group, a gym, or a religious institution, then get them. It is not selfish to remember your life before parenting. Your life is not over with the birth of your child, no matter their level of need. Look to yourself as your child's greatest resource. Husband that resource like you would any other. Don't waste it.

Training

Do not confuse reading this book with attendance at good IDEA trainings. There are important things that are unique to your state, community, and even school.

The only way I know for you to learn and master these is to find and attend quality IEP trainings in your community or get involved in some serious networking with other parents. Each phase of your child's educational life has a different emphasis. Master them one at a time. Don't be afraid to ask questions.

Over 6 million American children are receiving educational services on IEPs. We are a powerful force. You are not alone.

This book gives you information and, as we know, information is power.

Cultivate, along with power, a sense of humor. It will go a long way when things are at their bleakest.

Never stop learning.

Chapter Two

PRESCHOOL CHILDREN

"Where have you been, my blue eyed son?
Oh, where have you been, my darling young one?"

Bob Dylan

Where Were You?

My parents' generation asked, "Where were you when the news of Pearl Harbor came?" For my generation the question was, "Where were you when the news of President Kennedy's death was announced?" For my children the question is "Where were you when you heard about 9/11?"

For each generation, the question is about a monumental, life-changing event. Before you read this chapter on early childhood, take a moment to ask yourself, "Where was I when I learned my child had a disability?" Put your memory to work and recall who told you, where you were, what people wore, what the weather was like, who was there? Mostly remember your first reaction.

That moment is a good place to start thinking about early childhood services. You have come a long way since that first moment. Think about all of the things you have learned. Realize how much stronger you are now and all of the new and frightening things you have already overcome.

We all have a story. Here is ours. Use it to remember yours.

How We Met Eleanor

"Your daughter has an extra chromosome," said the man in the surgical mask. "It is called Down syndrome and, if you're interested, there is some literature you can read before you leave the hospital,"

That is how our family was introduced to the world of disability and special education. Eleanor was fifteen minutes old. Fifteen minutes is how much time we were allotted to meet the brilliant, beautiful, "normal" child we had expected. And fifteen minutes is enough time for excitement to turn to panic and fear. In that time, the imagined child we had just met evaporated. We were too innocent at the time to know that this "new" child was just the right one for us. Fifteen minutes is, at once, a heart-stoppingly long and a breathlessly short time.

Every family has its own story. Ours is only different from yours in one way. It happened to us.

On April 2, 1988, at 7 o-clock in the morning, there was no subject on earth that I knew less about then Down syndrome and developmental disabilities. The sound of the sobbing delivery room nurses didn't help.

"Is this serious?" I asked one of them. "Yes," she said. "It is very serious."

In my confusion I visualized an adult, helpless in a bed in a shaded room that smelled of medicine and antiseptic. In the vision, her mother and I were old and leaning wearily over the bed.

"Will she ever walk?" I asked. "Yes, she will walk," replied the weeping nurse. "But she won't do much more."

Jonna, Eleanor's mother, was recovering from Caesarian delivery just inches away from this conversation. "It's alright," I said to her in my most unconvincing voice.

She looked back and said, "No, it isn't."

During that day, a network of friends put me in touch with a woman who has an adult daughter with Down syndrome. Her name was

Marguerite. I called her and, oddly, began pouring out my feelings to her, a stranger. I never met her and never spoke to her again. She said the wisest thing anyone has ever said about Eleanor. "Mr. Bailey," she said, "enjoy her babyhood."

I did.

Eleanor was underweight and unable to maintain her body temperature. She went to the Neo-Natal Intensive Care ward and that night I sat with her and she instinctively wrapped her little baby finger around my hand and I fell in love in a way I had not known was possible.

I know now that when an infant's palm is stroked its fingers instinctively close. This is known in medicine as the Palmer Grasp. It is one of those natural devices that bond parents and children. Instinct or not, it worked on me. I loved the feeling of that little hand clutching my finger.

She stared at me and I stared back at her. She looked perfect to me.

"There is lots of room in my life for you," I told her. "Your mom and I will always love you and we will be the best parents we can be and you will have a good and happy life." Two years later, when her sister was born, that promise was repeated. That is a promise we intend to keep.

Some friends were unbelievably loving and helpful. Some acted like we had experienced the death of a child and not the birth. Our families were wonderful. They accepted their new granddaughter and niece with open hearts. Their concern was what this would mean to their own children's lives, the lives of Eleanor's parents. None of us had yet learned that it wasn't about our lives, it was about hers.

Her maternal grandfather, John, a professor of surgery, went straight to his colleagues and learned all about Down syndrome and heart problems. Talking to him and getting some real information was the first step toward empowering us as parents. It helped us come back from the abyss of fear and ignorance and know what to say and what to ask when we talked with her doctors. It turned out that Eleanor's heart was fine. Although we didn't know it at the time we were one of the lucky ones. Her life did not begin with heart surgery the way the lives of so many babies with Down syndrome do.

Four days later we took her home and laid her down in a garden of blossoming spring tulips and took her picture. She was all swaddled and pink and smiling and beautiful. It seemed impossible that there was anything wrong with her.

At least she was finally home and in the little nursery that had been painted and furnished just for her. It hadn't occurred to us that there would be any help, any program that would focus on us and help us to understand our daughter and the things we would need to know to keep our promise to her and to ourselves.

Happily, Eleanor's Uncle Matt was a special education high school transition specialist with our local school district. He had lots of connections in a world I scarcely knew existed, the world of service delivery. "If you're going to have a disability," he said, "Down syndrome is the one to have."

What Are Early Intervention Services?

Early intervention services for children birth-to-three are services "designed to meet the developmental needs of children with disabilities and the needs of the family related to enhancing the child's development." These services take on a very personal feel when they respect the traditions and values of your own family. The way you wish to raise your child, what things matter to you, customs, holidays, and even dress can be very important to you. These services must reflect what matters to your family.

We learned that examples of early intervention services are things like speech therapy and associated issues, family training, special instruction, social work services, physical therapy, counseling and home visits, occupational therapy, service coordination, etc. When you see a need in your child, you simply figure out a way to get it within one of the "set" service categories, put it in a plan, and, presto, it is provided. Or at least it is supposed to work that way.

In our case, it did.

When Eleanor was about six weeks old we had a home visit arranged by Uncle Matt. Three women from our county developmental disabilities services division came to our house. They gave us some information and some comforting words. Unbeknownst to us they did an "evaluation" of Eleanor. They let us know that we were eligible for a service called "Early Intervention."

We were asked to make a choice between three available programs. (Since 1988 Oregon's budget has changed so dramatically for the worse that parents today are offered one program that they can take or leave.) For no particular reason we chose a non-profit provider and soon were introduced to our "consultant."

It was decided that I would shut down my law practice and stay home with Eleanor for a year. Her mother, after her maternity leave, would return to her own law practice. This turned out to be a great decision for me. It was one of the best years of my life. What a privilege for a male to be the primary care giver to an infant human. Eleanor and I had a great time!

One of the reasons it was such a good year was the weekly visit of our early intervention "consultant." She was a font of knowledge, practical advice, reality tips, and a window into the real world. I learned about things like low muscle tone and how to teach a baby to sit up and get back on the floor without simply flopping its torso onto the carpet. I learned that even infants could have abhorrence for work.

Raelyn, our consultant, told us about stimulation and colors and contrasts. Soon the house and car were awash in images in black and white. Music was a good thing for brain development, she told us. For one year, five days a week, Eleanor and I snuggled on the couch and listened to Mozart's "Requiem." We built fires, we cooked, we rolled around, we laughed and I got to play like I had not played since my own childhood. I became very good at changing diapers and dealing with formula. When mom came home we proudly showed her the remnants of our latest obstacle course or how those little fingers could pluck the strings of my guitar.

We passed a whole year like that. Me, oblivious to notions like developmental delay; Eleanor growing and cooing and turning over, and her mom coming home from work to prepared dinners and a clean kid. All of us started learning sign language because someone told us it was a good communication tool, since Eleanor would not learn to talk at a typical time.

We had the best services we could imagine and they were delivered in the best possible way. Nice people caring about our child and us. We knew nothing about rules, regulations, budgets or administrators. We were the happy family that the people who invented Early Intervention imagined.

Alas, all good things must end!

At the end of that year our home visits were suddenly restricted and we learned that services would now be provided with other "kids like her," in a church basement, miles away. It seems odd now, but that was the first time it occurred to me that there was this great structure out there that was making decisions for us.

There were suddenly, looming before us like an unknown and unexpected behemoth, important decisions to be made. It was a profound awakening.

And that is how it began for us.

A Short History of Early Intervention and Early Childhood Special Education

Our family benefited richly from a complex web of laws, regulations, and organizations that came together in the past to do some serious organizing and political work to create a national early childhood education program. That program made our first year possible.

Since then I have complained about the quality and focus of services. But I am profoundly aware that in the years before Eleanor's birth, other parents saw some needs and created for those of us who came afterwards a system that, at its best, works wonderfully. Even at its worst, it is a revolutionary change for the better. An historical perspective is helpful during those seemingly inevitable days when our anger toward education professionals reaches, and sometimes exceeds, the boiling point.

Prior to the 1980s there was no federal policy that set a national agenda for children with disabilities. Educational opportunity, if any, differed not only from state to state but also town to town and even from neighborhood to neighborhood.

In the 1950s parents of kids with disabilities bonded together to attempt to create some educational and social opportunities for their children with disabilities. Many of these first attempts took place in the basements of churches. There were no publicly funded budgets to fret about, and teachers, to the extent there were any, were volunteers. Little attention was paid to the needs of newborns and their families. The attention focused on school-age children.

The Education of the Handicapped Act (EHA) dealt exclusively with the education of school age children with disabilities. On October 8, 1986, Public Law 99-457 amended the EHA to include, for the first time, a national agenda intended to improve, standardize, and increase services for young children with disabilities, birth to five. The amendments also required the services to be focused not just on the needs of the children but also on the needs of the entire family.

The law officially recognized the unique role of families in the development of their children, along with giving families the legal right to participate in all aspects of the service providing process. The importance of that fact cannot be overemphasized.

The amendments made us equal decision-making partners at every step. We do not attend meetings because a sensitive professional invited us to observe. We are there because the law requires it. It is our right. It is a right to protect and exercise at every opportunity.

Service planning meetings for birth-to-five children are known as Individual Family Service Plans (IFSP). They are intended to serve families. They have rules and limitations and you have the right to be thoroughly informed about every one of them. You have the right to have your individual family values and hopes respected and included in your family plan. The law was never intended to be a "one-size-fits-all" offering. It is about serving one family at a time.

Special Education Law and Young Children - the 1997 Amendments to IDEA

The basic federal law granting and protecting the educational rights of children with disabilities is the Individuals with Disabilities Education Act (IDEA). In 1986 (PL 99-457), 1990, and again in 1991, IDEA was amended to include early childhood reforms. During the IDEA reauthorization of 1997, considerable change was made that strengthened the role of families.

Currently IDEA contains three areas that are especially relevant to infants, toddlers, and preschoolers. Those are Part C. Section 619 of Part B and the Early Education Program for Children with Disabilities. (EEPCD).

Part C – Infants and Toddlers with Disabilities Program

Part C is the section of IDEA that creates Early Intervention. Early Intervention services are those provided from birth to age three. The federal role is to assist states in planning, developing, funding, and implementing a statewide system of comprehensive, coordinated, and multidisciplinary interagency programs for all young children from birth to three years.

After a child's third birthday they move into another legislative scheme called Early Childhood Special Education (ECSE). These services are provided under what is commonly called Section 619.

Some states' have adopted a "seamless system," meaning that the two sections of the law are administered together so that families really don't know, or have any reason to know, that they have moved from one service delivery model to another.

The Individual Family Support Plan implements services to your family. But it is only one portion of the whole early childhood agenda. Most of us don't know, or care, about the rest. Nevertheless, it can be useful to have an overall view of the whole early childhood agenda; here is a summary of what a statewide system must look like.

The law requires states' to design a service delivery system that is family centered, responsive to family needs, collaborative, culturally competent, and of high quality. There must be an emphasis on natural settings. Just how these concepts are defined, and the role of state budgets in defining them, varies from year to year and state to state. For parent advocates the most important value is the requirement of "natural settings." Ideally services to infants and toddlers will take place in the home or, at least, the neighborhood. This is a reflection of Early Intervention policy that is weighted toward serving one family at a time.

Part B requires a state plan to include these components.

- A definition of developmentally delayed.
- A timetable to assure appropriate service for all eligible children.

- A multidisciplinary evaluation.
- Case management to accompany the IFSP.
- A comprehensive child find and referral system.
- A public awareness program.
- A central directory of services, resources, and research.
- A plan for personnel development.
- A single line of authority.
- A policy for timely reimbursement of funds.
- Procedural safeguards.
- A statewide policy that includes procedures for personnel standards.
- A system for compiling data.

A lead agency is named by the Governor to carry out the planning and implementation of Early Intervention in each state. Typically, though not always, the lead agency is the state Department of Education. The lead agency is responsible for general supervision and administration of the state's program. Because services are collaborative, the lead agency must find and identify all available resources in order to avoid duplication and creation of unnecessary new programs. Financial responsibility and the adoption of procedures to ensure services are also handled by this agency. Lastly, the lead agency contracts with local providers for the actual provision of services. (Budgets for IE/ECSE are separate from general education budgets.)

Each state is required to organize an Interagency Coordinating Council (ICC) to advise and assist the lead agency. The Governor appoints members of the ICC. The ICC is composed of agency representatives, service providers, university programs, and parents. Being a parent member of your state's ICC is a rewarding and educational experience for a new parent. It is also an excellent way to introduce you to the personalities and systems that will come to bear on your child when they enter school.

Welcome to FAPE!
Early Childhood Special Education
(Part B – Section 619)

As I earlier noted, this part is commonly referred to as Section 619. Early Childhood Special Education (ECSE) is provided to children from age three to five.

Please note, though, that the previously detailed Part C is an optional program for states, not a requirement. States choose to participate because of an allotment of federal funds that help them implement early intervention. Section 619, however, is mandatory.

When a child is three years old he or she are considered a preschooler. At this stage your family is moving closer to the reality of IDEA. One of the most important IDEA rights is a Free and Appropriate Public Education (FAPE). This is an entitlement that children with disabilities enjoy until the end of the school year following their 21st birthday. But it begins at age three.

Although your services will continue to be administered through the IFSP, the administrative structure has changed. Instead of services being provided in "natural environments" the requirement is called "least restrictive environment" and reflects what you will become used to during Individual Education Program (IEP) meetings in future. All of the IDEA safeguards and rules, including Due Process, IEPs and placements, apply to ECSE.

Federal funds are provided to each state to assist in implementing these programs.

Early Education Program for Children with Disabilities (EEPCD)

The last of the three IDEAS mandated services to infants, toddlers, and preschoolers is EEPCD. The purpose of EEPCD is to provide states with support in the development and implementation of their Part C and Section 619 service systems.

Today there are nearly 150 EEPCD projects scattered around the country. These centers often sponsor "demonstration projects" based on new research. They also do research, provide in-service training for personnel and parents, and support statewide data system development and technical assistance.

One EEPCD project of particular importance to families is the National Early Education Technical Assistance System (NEC*TAS). This project, with its admittedly bulky title, supports all other EEPCD projects and offers annual trainings and conferences that families are encouraged to attend. Most parent members of their state ICC will have the
opportunity to attend at least one of these meetings during their term. The sessions are a wonderful chance to learn more about how services are provided on a national level and, of most importance, a first opportunity to meet other parents from different parts of the country and begin the process of building a personal network that will serve you well in years to come.

A good resource for more information on federal policy and early childhood services is the Frank Porter Graham Child Development Center, University of North Carolina at Chapel Hill.

Service Referrals

For some time I felt quite unhappy with the brutal way we were told of our daughter's disability. But, with the passage of time, I have come to feel that we were lucky to learn about Eleanor's disability in the delivery room. Many families celebrate the birth of what appears to be a normal child. The child goes home and months or, sometimes, years go by before parents begin to wonder about some curious trait or apparent developmental delay. None of us want to see that kind of problem in our child. Often the situation becomes so acute that physicians are the ones to speak the truth to frightened, nervous parents who don't want to hear it.

But eventually even the most reluctant of us will do what we decide is best for our child. The label of disability is something that makes people afraid. All of us, at least at first, would like to run away from it.

Our family had no time to get used to the idea of a "normal" child. We were already processing information about her disability when we brought her home from the hospital. But for people who are surprised by a diagnosis when their child is age three or older, the shock must be worse, and the referral and evaluation process, a very difficult and confusing time. But for every family that dreads the label of disability, there is another family so desperate for information and help that the evaluation is a time of relief and hope.

In order to be eligible for services, a child must be evaluated. The most common method of finding your way into service is to receive a referral from a physician. The details vary from state to state but every state requires local agencies to have a "designated referral and evaluation agency." The agency is responsible for both finding children in need of services and evaluating them. The exact agency information in your community is available from school districts, the state department of education, hospitals, churches, and other social service agencies. In the absence of a referral you may call the evaluation agency and schedule an evaluation.

Once a referral is made to an evaluating agency, each state has a rule about how quickly the evaluation must take place. Check the rules of your state's lead agency or ask the referral person or evaluator. Emphasis is on speed. Once a child is suspected of being eligible for service, the law encourages quick resolution so that needed services may begin as soon as possible.

What Is an Evaluation?

An evaluation leads to a label, and a label is what you need to get services now and forever. "Label jars, not people," is a disability rights slogan that makes sense. But services can't happen without a label. This is a dilemma for parents trying to instill in their children a sense of intrinsic worth as a human being. None of us want to be known simply as a label. I think being a parent of a child with a disability is more art than science. Labels and diagnoses are part of our lives. Unfortunately, we simply have to get over it.

Most states allow an "informed clinical opinion" to approve eligibility for early childhood services. Sometimes a physician does the evaluation but, more commonly, by agency personnel.

Early Intervention (EI) is governed, as we know, by Part C. Early Childhood Special Education (ECSE) is provided under Title 619. Eligibility can be determined in two ways, and it is to be expected that each program would have slightly different eligibility criteria.

For children birth-to-three, the first method is a determination of whether or not the child falls within one or more specific criteria of **developmental delay**. The categories are: Cognitive development; physical development, including vision and hearing; communication development, social or emotional development; adaptive development. The lead agency of your state has definitions of these categories. An easy way to find them is by using the Internet.

The second method of eligibility for children birth-to-three is a medical diagnosis of a physical or mental condition which has a high probability or resulting in a developmental delay.

For children age three to five, who will be receiving ECSE services under Title 619 the evaluation, is a little different. Children in this age range must have a substantial developmental delay (states define this differently) in TWO or more of the following areas: cognitive, physical, communication, social or emotional, adaptive; OR meet eligibility criteria for a specific listed disabling condition. Those conditions are: autism, blindness, deaf and blind, hearing impairment, mental retardation, orthopedic impairment, communication disorder, emotional disturbance, specific learning disability, "other health impairment," traumatic brain injury and visual impairment.

Another difference in an ECSE evaluation is that two trained people must do it. One of them must be trained in the specific suspected disability and the other must be from a different discipline. The composition of these teams is the responsibility of the evaluation agency.

It is important for families to accept the fact that diagnosis and labeling are a prerequisite for services for your child's whole life. None of us like them. But your child's label is just there to start a money trail for services that have a high probability of improving your child's and your family's life and future. Learn to laugh about it. The kids do.

Eleanor is now a teenager. She and her pals with Down syndrome refer to themselves as "Downers." This may not satisfy the politically correct "people first language" crowd, but it strikes me as indicative of the kind of relief these kids feel when they are with each other and learning how to create a bond of friendship that is uniquely their own.

Our children are all unique. Our children are not their labels. Parents must learn to believe that, and they must teach it to their child. People with disabilities are human beings more like "normal" people than different. The system, sadly, runs on labeling. How much better it would be if we provided whatever supports every child, regardless of ability or disability, needs, and abandon labels. Alas, we are a long way from that dream.

Once your child is found eligible, the next step is the development of an IFSP. That plan will direct and detail exactly what services are needed and which ones will be provided.

Individual Family Service Plans (IFSP)

The IFSP is a written plan developed at a meeting. The completed plan describes in detail the services to be provided, who will provide them and the expected outcomes of those services. If the service is in the plan, you may expect it to happen. A service not in the plan will not be provided. These meetings are important.

The actual meetings must be scheduled at a place and time convenient for families.

The IFSP must describe goals and objectives in detail. Once your goals are established the document lists the services you will need in order to meet the goals. The IFSP must be implemented as soon as possible after the meeting, although no services can be provided without your written consent.

The IFSP must be reviewed every six months and sooner if you ask for it. The purpose of a review is to look at progress on the goals and to see whether or not it is necessary to changes, goals, outcomes, or placements.

The document is good for one calendar year and must be renewed. The meeting must take place unless you agree to an alternate format, such as a telephone call or written update.

What Is Included in an IFSP?

The precise composition of an IFSP may vary slightly from state to state, but here is an overview that will address most of the common elements.

The first thing that must be included is a classic special education acronym, a PLOP. That means Present Level of Performance and will be used in all IFSP and IEP meetings. It is simply a basis to determine a starting point for writing goals and objectives. The PLOP is the base on which the plan is built.

The specific services necessary to meet the unique needs of the child must be included.

In our case, we had decided that Eleanor would, more or less, develop physically. We were more concerned with the label of mental retardation and wanted to emphasize intellectual stimulation. One of the means we chose was to look at ways to help her communicate.

We chose American Sign Language. With the help of our consultant, we began to learn sign language and teach the signs to Eleanor. She was two years old when we began and was talking little or, truthfully, not at all.

She responded beautifully and before long we all knew nearly one-hundred signs. It was a modest amount compared to families with a deaf or hard-of-hearing child, but it opened a whole new world for the three of us. Eleanor retained and expanded the use of signing. Today she can sign at the speed of a certified sign language interpreter.

We also wanted her to talk and talk plainly. Early Intervention and Early Childhood Special Education services are designed to be collaborative. The point of that is to save the expense of establishing a service, such as speech therapy, when such services are available from existing community agencies.

As part of our IFSP we set a goal that she would learn a certain number of words and use and pronounce them correctly. The method for achieving the goal was one hour a week of private speech therapy paid for by our private insurance policy. Her progress was monitored by the team but paid for by insurance. This is an example of a collaborative approach, which takes into account family resources and team expertise. Of course, if we had not had the insurance, she still would have gotten the speech therapy but from a different provider and at public expense. This is true because the goal was written into the IFSP.

The team felt that additional speech therapy in a different setting, with other kids, would help to achieve her speech goals and her socialization goals. For two summers she attended twice weekly, four-hour sessions at the Portland Center for Speech and Hearing. That too was a great success. That was a service paid for by Early Intervention.

Ultimately our insurance company paid for sixty sessions of private therapy. Eleanor was so attached to her therapist that we privately paid him to come to our home twice a month for an additional year. These sessions, our constant talking to her and patiently awaiting her response, and the Portland Center for Speech and Hearing sessions resulted in her being able to speak very clearly and develop a normal vocabulary of words. By the time she was four she could carry on a conversation with anyone. But, NOTE TO PARENTS, be careful what you wish for. As will be seen in our discussion of placements, sometimes your child's skill and your words may return to haunt you.

Additional formal requirements for an IFSP include the dates when services will begin and end; a clear description of which person or agency is responsible for providing the service; a description of who is responsible for implementing the plan; steps to support transition of the child from EI to ECSE and from ECSE to kindergarten.

What Is Placement?

The IFSP team determines what specific services are necessary to meet the "unique needs" of the child. The team also decides placement, or where the services will be provided. Parents are part of the placement-deciding team.

Again, allow for some variance from state to state, but the IFSP team, for EI, is composed of:

- The parents of the child.
- Other family members if requested by the parents.
- An advocate or person from outside the family, if requested by the parents.
- The service coordinator.
- The early intervention specialist or related services personnel serving the child.
- Other individuals at the discretion of the parents, contracting agency.
- A member of the evaluation team.
- The IFSP team for ECSE meetings is similar but slightly different.

It includes:
- Parents – who are always required at any special education meeting that concerns their child.
- The child's ECSE teacher or specialist.
- A contractor who is qualified to provide or supervise services.
- Others invited by the parents or contractor.
- For the first IFSP, a member of the evaluation team; and
- For the first IFSP meeting the year before the child enters school, a representative of the school district.

Decisions of the IFSP team cannot be changed unless parents are given written notice at least ten days prior to any proposed change in eligibility, services or placement. The notice must include a description of the proposed change, reasons for the change, other options considered and rejected, and a clear description of the parents' rights to contest the change.

What Sorts of Preschool Placements Are Available?

The type, level and location of services to families of children birth-to-three (EI) are different from services to children three-to-five (ECSE).

Services for EI

For EI children, services must be provided in "natural environments" to the "maximum extent appropriate." Parents, please note, this is not the same as "maximum extent possible." These services are intended to be individual services to one child at a time. The provider's budget issues are not your problem while you are advocating for your child's future. It is not uncommon for providers to locate more and more restrictive placements because of budget issues and then confuse "appropriate" with "possible." If what is appropriate is home services, then home services are what you are entitled to.

EI kids from birth to age two are entitled to a service coordinator and that coordinator may be provided through age three. This coordinator must be recognized as having special skill and knowledge about infants and toddlers with disabilities, EI laws and regulations, and service options.

A service coordinator, as a designated "rights protector" has mandated duties.
Among those duties are:

- Assist the child and family in receiving the rights and procedural safeguards required by law.
- Inform the family of the availability of advocacy services, such as the state Protection and Advocacy agency and Parent Training and Information Centers.
- The coordinator must assist the child and family in getting services in a timely manner.
- Serve as a single point of contact for parents to get help.
- Find service providers, and coordinate delivery of services.
- Coordinate evaluations.
- Facilitate and participate in the IFSP process.
- Coordinate with medical and health providers.
- Coordinate access to other services designated on the IFSP, including helping families apply for public benefits or special programs, prepare insurance claims and seek out and help to maintain needed health insurance.
- Continuously seek appropriate services necessary to assure that the child receives benefits during their eligibility.

Additionally, preschool children with mental retardation or another developmental disability may receive services through a state disabilities program. Eligibility is determined separately from the EI/ ECSE process. Check with a local advocacy organization for information on your state.

Services for ECSE

The IFSP focus for children three to five is on cognitive skills, self-help skills (including toileting), expressive and receptive language, and psychosocial development. The team must provide a preschool placement that will be most likely to address any specific concerns identified in the IFSP. The placement must be appropriate and free (FAPE).

It is also required that the preschool placement be, to the maximum extent "appropriate," with children who are not disabled. Placement options include programs operated by agencies other than contractors such as Head Start and public and private pre-kindergarten programs that provide services to all children. If the IFSP team places a child in a private preschool program, the entire educational program, including tuition, must be at no cost to the parents!

EI services are weighted toward being provided in "natural environments." ECSE introduces families, for the first time, to another special education practice with which you will become very familiar. Services must be provided in the "least restrictive environment." There is great emphasis on interaction with non-disabled peers. Placement in a location-serving child with disabilities exclusively will not be made unless "least restrictive environment" placements have been considered and rejected by the team.

Services must be provided as close as possible to the child's home, and transportation must be provided. Transportation must be provided for EI students and will be provided for ECSE students if it is necessary to participate in a related service, such as therapy or play sessions. In some states parents may opt out of bus and cab transportation and receive mileage reimbursement for providing necessary transportation.

The team must consider the array of services necessary to implement the IFSP, the level of supports needed by the child, and potential harmful effects on the child. Unless rejected by the team, services must be provided "in the types of settings in which children without disabilities would participate." In other words, services are not to be provided in hospitals, institutions, or clinics.

What About Medical Needs?

The IFSP contains a section called "other services." Medical services are not paid for by EI/ECSE funds. However, the IFSP should contain the steps that can be taken to assist your child in obtaining other funds for which they may be eligible, such as Medicaid or Supplemental Security Income (SSI).

For ECSE children, most states make a small exception to the rule that funds are not available for medical costs. Medical services that are solely for diagnostic or evaluation purposes are considered a "related service" and must be provided at district expense.

EI/ECSE Conflict Resolution

The precise procedures parents must follow in the event of disagreements about eligibility or services are detailed in state-by-state administrative rules. What is consistent everywhere is the obligation of your state to have such rules and the obligation of your service provider to make them available to you.

The best method of dispute resolution is the most informal one. If you have a dispute or disagreement, meet informally with program or contractor staff and work it out. Talk with them freely about your concerns and listen to their reasons for a decision. Often, what seems insurmountable can be solved by an honest conversation.

If an informal method does not work, you always have the right to call for an IFSP review. If you do this, be prepared to offer reasons why the current IFSP is not meeting your child's goals and why change is necessary.

In the case of ECSE children, you have the right to call for an independent evaluation. That is an evaluation done by someone not working for your provider. Your district or contractor must cover the cost of an independent evaluation.

In every state there are procedures to try to resolve conflict. They are discussed in more detail in the chapter on IEPs. These conflict resolution mechanisms are a combination of a request for formal mediation, a written complaint that must be investigated, and some kind of administrative hearing. Some states allow all three. These are called administrative remedies. Once you have used up your administrative remedies you may file a lawsuit.

Suing providers and districts is appropriate under certain conditions. I will warn you, however, that suits are expensive, protracted and always result in very hard feelings. Consult an experienced special education lawyer before taking, or threatening to take, this step.

Keep a Sense of Humor: Absurdities and Triumphs

Early childhood services for children with disabilities take place at a time when families are experiencing some of the most traumatic and frightening changes that can be imagined. None of us dreamed of becoming a parent of a child with a disability. Families are still in the process of accepting and learning to cherish a child they had never imagined would "happen to them." Your feelings are natural and this is a good time to test them. It is also a good time to start developing skills that you will need for the rest of your life.

IFSP meetings have the power to do a lot of things and provide a lot of services. But they are governed by rules and sometimes the rules and common sense collide is startling ways. Persistence and a sense of humor are more apt to result in success than rancor.

Learning new rules, terminology, and ways of thinking are essential. Developing networks with other families, and learning to have a healthy relationship with professionals of all kinds is also essential. Additionally, you, your partner, and your closest family members need to be able to step back a bit and have a sense of humor about all of this. Call it black humor if you want. The healing power of a good laugh goes a long way.

The IFSP we did when Eleanor was four years old is a classic example of rules gone wild. It also shows how surprised you can be by what your child, perhaps unknown to you, has learned.

Looking around for a good program for her fourth year, we visited and chose a site called the "West Hills Montessori School." There was a classroom there of typical four year olds, an experienced teacher, and a predominance of non-disabled children. It seemed perfect.

We brought that suggestion to the IFSP team. The team enthusiastically endorsed the program. We wrote up the plan, the team made the placement decision and it was decided that the district would pay for a cab to come to our house each morning and take Eleanor to and from her half-day preschool program.

A few days later the phone rang and our service coordinator said, "We cannot provide transportation for Eleanor to the West Hills Montessori School."

Taken aback, we asked "Why not?"

"Because," she replied, "it is in another county and the rules would not allow us to transport anyone out of the county."

Portland, Oregon, like all other American cities has grown out of its original boundaries and merged with what were once suburban communities separated from the city by farms and highways. All of us on the IFSP team assumed that the school was in Multnomah County. But, alas, it is in Washington, County, just barely.

Olsen Road runs north and south through that part of the city. It is a four lane arterial with lots of traffic. The east side is Multnomah County and the west side is Washington County. Less than 100 feet separate one side of the street from the other.

What happened next is a good example of how families and professionals can, given the right attitude, work together to make things happen for a child.

The rather sheepish service coordinator offered to have the cab drive Eleanor to a business called The Red Tomato Pizza Company. It was located on the corner of Olsen Road and Capitol Highway. The driver would help Eleanor out of the car and she would have to walk across the street by herself to complete her trip. We requested some time to think about it.

We called the school and asked if they could have someone meet Eleanor and help her cross the road. They were sympathetic but had no staff to do that.

So we were left with the idea of a four-year-old girl with Down syndrome and a big backpack navigating a busy intersection alone. Obviously we were not going to let that happen.

We called a meeting. The district people restated their happiness with the placement and explained again how they could not do the transportation. Eleanor's mom and I looked at her and began to laugh. She looked at us and she laughed. Soon we all laughed. It was too absurd. An important placement was going to be lost because a cab could not drive an extra hundred feet.

We agreed that the cab would drive the extra hundred feet. We agreed that it would not be in the plan. We agreed not to talk about it. The result was a wonderful year for Eleanor, a wonderful friendship with Tom the cab driver who became a fast family friend and the cementing of some real trust with our service provider.

That year was a fabulous conclusion to our early childhood experiences.

How It Ended for Us

Eleanor's teacher was an experienced professional with all kinds of skills. Her classroom was remarkably decorous considering all of the four-year-olds in it. The kids were well behaved, knew what was expected, raised their hands when they needed something, and were an exemplary group of boys and girls.

The last week of school, the class was involved with growing little plants in clay pots, the little red ones that can be purchased at any nursery and placed in a matching plate to catch the dirt and excess water. A proud child was showing her project to the attentive class when she accidentally dropped the pot onto the floor. Predictably it noisily broke into dozens of shards of pottery and the dirt flew everywhere.

"Oooooo," said some children. "Ahhhhhh," said others. "Oops," said some more.

"Fuck!" said Eleanor.

The teacher was appalled at such language and let me know that when I hastened to obey her summons to the school. But as she recited the horror of the event, I could not help but be very proud.

"She was so clear," said the teacher.

I thought to myself, "All of those hours of speech therapy are paying off."

At the end of her eligibility for early childhood services, Eleanor had pronounced and properly used a common piece of American vernacular in an appropriate setting. What more could we ask?

Our efforts had been a success! We turned our attention to the many new adventures that lay ahead in big-time special education.

Chapter 3

SCHOOL-AGE CHILDREN

"An IEP is when a bunch of grownups get together and say mean things about me."

Eleanor Bailey
Student and Commentator

The Heart and Soul of Services
Part I
A foundation in law
What is Special Education?
What Are Related Services?
What is Assistive Technology?
Part II
Who is Eligible for Special Education?
Eligibility under IDEA
Eligibility under Section 504
"Accommodation" under Section 504
Evaluation and Parental Rights
Part III
Lesson #1: The IEP Drives Your Services
Additional Parental Rights
Part IV
What is an IEP Team?
The IEP Content
Transition to Adult Life
Regular Education, Standardized Tests and Assessments
Measurements, Reviews and Modifications
Good, Bad and Ugly

The Heart and Soul of Services

An Individual Education Program, or IEP, is the heart and soul of service delivery to eligible children, age five to twenty-one. Mastering the art of writing and implementing your child's IEP is a parent's most important task. It seems daunting. Be patient with yourself. Take it one step at a time.

The IEP meeting is the time of year when those most concerned with, and responsible for, the child's school experience sit down and make a plan. Because each child's individual needs are different, each plan is different. Each plan is developed to meet the educational needs of one child at a time. "Special" education means specially designed curriculum created to address the needs of a single student. Remember the basics; keep the child at the center of all discussion.

This is a wonderful concept. It is a concept that should be applied to all students, whether or not they have a disability. But, like many other good and simple ideas, this one has become a flash point for stress, conflict, and emotional turmoil and, often, a breakdown in parent-educator communication, mutual confidence and trust. In other words, an IEP meeting can be a nightmare.

Parents want the very best educational program for their child. Parents want the state of the art educational plan. Schools are not required to provide anything more that what is adequate to guarantee "meaningful progress." And there lies the rub; the difference between what we want and what they are required to provide. School administrators, naturally, want to control cost. Parents want the best possible program.

The challenge of IEP advocacy is to design a program that families are happy with and the school is willing to implement. Don't be deceived into thinking the school is "required" to implement the program. That statement is true in a legal sense, but in a day-to-day sense, it is best to "move heaven and earth" to get them to buy in. Forcing compliance can be done, but, in the real world, it is neither practical nor desirable.

Eleanor's reaction, quoted above, is her description of what it felt like to her to attend one of her own meetings. Many parents and educators have characterized the experience in much stronger language.

It does not have to be this way.

The IEP drives your child's services. If an educational service is in the IEP you can expect it happen. If the services are not in the IEP, the school has no obligation to provide it. This is the most important single fact you need to know. The creation and implementation of an IEP is the one indispensable skill you need.

The first things you need to learn are the basic principles and rules. There is a lot to know. Don't expect to learn it all quickly. Learn what you need to know. The skills you need to make the transition from kindergarten to first grade are not the same as the ones you need to make the transition to adulthood. Worry about what's on your plate right now. There will be time to learn the rest. Start with the basics.

PART 1
A Foundation in Law

The Individuals with Disabilities Education Act (IDEA) is the federal law designed especially for children with disabilities. The law requires that each state provide a "free and appropriate public education" (FAPE) to every child found to have a disability. The "free" part is easy to understand. Every eligible child has the right to receive instruction at no cost to the parents or guardians of the child. "Appropriate" means specially designed curriculum that meets the individual educational needs of the child.

IDEA applies to children with disabilities who require specially designed instruction. But there are other children with disabilities who may have that need but, nevertheless, need some special assistance. What about them?

Section 504 of the federal Vocational Rehabilitation Act protects those children's rights. Section 504 makes it illegal to discriminate against an "otherwise qualified" person on the basis of disability. It is not specifically an education law but, rather, prohibits discrimination in any activity or program that receives funds from the federal government. Since all school districts receive federal funds, the requirements of Section 504 apply to them.

Section 504 requires that a person with a disability be able to participate in programs and activities available to people without disabilities. This means that schools must make "accommodations" for the student's disability so that he or she can participate in general education classes and other school activities.

Most states use a standard IEP form for development of a FAPE for students covered by IDEA and the accommodations requirement of Section 504. Thus the skills required are similar for each law.

Whether you are using IDEA or Section 504 there are fundamental things you will need to know. These are things you will use throughout your child's life as a special education student.

What Is Special Education?

IDEA defines special education as instruction which is specially designed to meet the unique needs of a child with a disability, and is provided at no cost to the parents.

The IEP you will design must be created to meet the individual needs of your child. A "one size fits all" educational program is not special education and will not meet the legal requirements for an IEP. Districts have great temptation to place special education students in designed programs to serve a category of eligibility. "This is our Down syndrome program," is the kind of statement, for example, that does not meet the requirements of the law. Within categories of eligibility the law recognizes that each child's needs are unique, and it requires the school to recognize that as well.

The requirement of a handcrafted program that meets the unique needs of each child is so strong that special education services may be provided not only in a classroom but also in the child's home, a hospital, institution, or other setting, as needed.

Your right to have an individual plan for your child's individual need is the first and most important thing you need to know about IEP advocacy. Often school personnel are stressed, overworked, and exhausted. It is natural that they would prefer one plan for a category of children. Your best defense against that drift at an IEP meeting is a single sentence.

"We know and appreciate how hard you work and how many children you are responsible for. But this meeting is only about *Susan's* educational plan."

Apply your knowledge of the law to keep things on track. Special education is about educating one child at a time!

What Are "Related Services?"

An IEP sets out the educational goals for the child. Related services are services listed in the IEP that assure that the child will receive educational benefit from the plan. Related services are not actual instruction but, rather, the services a child needs to make the program work for him or her. Related services that a child needs in order to receive a free and appropriate public education (remember FAPE) must be provided at no cost to the parents.

A child who is a wheelchair user may require special transportation to get to and from school. Put simply, the IEP will be of no use if the child can't get to school.

Providing a vehicle with a wheelchair lift is an example of a related service. A child who has severe emotional behaviors that make it impossible for he or she to attend classes and participate in school activities may require psychological counseling. The counseling is a related service. Note that the counseling, like the wheelchair accessible transportation, is not an education service in itself. But it is a service necessary to make the FAPE requirement meaningful.

There are lessons here for parent advocates. Use your knowledge of that simple principle we call a FAPE. Your focus is on "appropriate." Related services are what make the plan work in practice. They are appropriate. They are required.

Some examples of related services include, but are not limited, to the following.

- Speech therapy and hearing services.
- Transportation.
- Physical and occupational therapy.
- Counseling.
- Social work services.
- School health services.
- Recreational services.
- Medical services for diagnosis and evaluation.
- Parent counseling and training.
- Psychological services.
- Rehabilitation.

Providing related services to meet a child's special education needs may require the use of special equipment or products. In order to meet the "appropriate" requirement of FAPE, it is sometimes necessary to provide items so that a child may perform a task necessary to meet his or her educational goals. This category of equipment and products is known as "assistive technology."

What Is Assistive Technology?

Your child has the right to the assistive technology products and devices that are identified in the IEP. Common examples of assistive technology include:

- Computers and modified computer equipment such as large keyboards or special screens.
- Computer programs that "speak" to the user.
- Medical equipment, including nursing services, for people with breathing difficulties or other medical condition.
- Closed-caption screens on television sets and computers.
- Teletype (TTY) devices that enable people with hearing loss to use the telephone.
- Assistance in note taking, such as tape recorders.
- Computer keyboards adapted for people with limited use of their hands.

Assistive technology has two operative definitions you should know.

"Assistive technology device" is defined by IDEA as a piece of equipment, or a product system, that is used to increase, maintain, or improve the capabilities of a child with a disability to function in school.

An "assistive technology service" is any service that helps a child with a disability to select, obtain, or use an assistive technology device or product.

The assistive technology service that your child may be entitled to includes:

- An evaluation of the child's need for assistive technology.
- Buying, leasing, or providing assistive technology devices.
- The selection, adaptation, repairing, fitting, or replacing of appropriate devices.
- The coordination of other services with assistive technology devices (related services such as therapy or counseling services).
- Providing training to the child or his or her family in learning how to use the devices properly and assisting with problems that may occur with daily use.
- Providing training to classroom teachers, related services providers, and therapists in the use of the assistive technology the child uses.

Assistive technology can be very complicated and expensive. It can also be something as simple as a custom stool or a simple communication aid. The use of assistive technology is of great importance. It is required because it is an appropriate service in order to guarantee educational benefit to the student. But for parents, it has the added value of preparing your child in the use of technology, computers, Internet, I-Pods, and assisted living programs currently available and under development, that will benefit them greatly as adults.

PART 2
Who Is Eligible for Special Education?

In order to receive special education and related services under IDEA or an "accommodation" under Section 504, your child must be found to be a "child with a disability." Your local school (called a "local education authority" or LEA) is responsible for making eligibility determinations. You have procedural rights regarding eligibility determination, which are discussed later in this chapter.

Eligibility standards for special education differ from those for a 504 plan. The differences are significant.

Eligibility for Special Education Under IDEA

Eligibility for special education services requires that your child meet one or more of the categories listed below. There are slight variations from state to state on precisely what that state means by each of these criteria. Although there are more similarities than differences you can check the exact criteria of your state by asking school personnel for the definitions or checking your state educational authority (SEA) website.

To qualify for special education and related services under federal law a child must fit into one of these categories AND need special education services.

First the categories:

- Mental retardation.
- Speech or language impairments.
- Emotional disturbance.
- Hearing impairments (including deafness).
- Orthopedic impairments including cerebral palsy, fractures or burns, bone diseases, etc.
- Autism spectrum disorders...some children with what are regarded as

"mild" forms of autism may not qualify for special education. (but can receive services under Section 504).
- Traumatic brain injury.
- Other health impairments, which may include such chronic or acute conditions as asthma, diabetes, epilepsy, cancer, and others.
- Specific learning disabilities. These are disabilities which are likely to impair the ability to learn, read, speak, write, spell, do math, etc. They also include conditions such as dyslexia or being non-verbal.

Normally a child who has one or more of these qualifying conditions will need special education services. But the law recognizes the possibility that there may be children who fit criteria and do not need the services. Thus, a child's need for services is the qualifying factor.

Eligibility for Services Under Section 504

Section 504 prohibits exclusion of children and adults from activities because of their disability. Remember, it is not an education act. It is an anti-discrimination law that protects the following people:

- Any person who has a physical or mental impairment that substantially limits one or more major life activities.
- Any person who has a record of such impairment.
- And person who is regarded as having such impairment.

Obviously these are terms that need some definition.

A "major life activity" includes the following:
- Seeing, sight, vision.
- Hearing, including being deaf or hard of hearing.
- Speaking, speech impairment, physical abnormalities that impact the ability to form words.
- Walking.
- Breathing.
- Learning.
- Working.
- Doing manual tasks that require motor skills.
- Self care skills such as hygiene, nutrition, money management, and personal safety.

Section 504 eligibility requires that the person have a significant limitation in some aspect of their life and that the limitation be the result of a physical or mental disability. An obvious example can be people with spinal bifida or cerebral palsy. Some of these individuals may not qualify for services under IDEA but will be entitled to an "accommodation" under Section 504 because of their mobility limitations. The same is true of mental disabilities, which may limit self-care skills and learning ability.

"Accommodation" Under Section 504

A Section 504 accommodation is any assistance or adaptation a student may need in order to participate in activities equally with other students who do not have a disability. Accommodation can mean help, aid, adjust, modify, support, etc.

One obvious Section 504 accommodation is making classrooms and school facilities accessible for wheelchair users and others with mobility limitations. Another is the use of alternative communication methods such as a specially designed computer keyboards, Braille, large type lessons or sign language.

For students with learning disabilities, Section 504 can require such things as oral testing, assistance in note taking, or modified and shortened writing assignments.

Another modification may be to require two sets of schoolbooks, one for school and one at home, to avoid having to carry them to and from. My daughter has this accommodation on her IDEA based IEP. She has a computer that she carries each day along with a communication notebook to facilitate our daily communication with her teachers. The addition of several high school text books makes it impossible for her to independently tote things to and from school.

An extra set of textbooks for home means that she can walk independently to and from high school. It seems simple. But it is a necessary accommodation that makes her FAPE have meaning.

There are, as we know, curious attitudes about disability. I was once asked to help a family in Astoria, Oregon. Their teenage daughter played on the high school soccer team. Oddly, the school district decided that because the young woman has autism it would be "unsafe" for her to continue to participate.

Educating the district on the irrelevance of autism to soccer and also reminding them that Section 504 affords people the right to accommodation when they are needed in order to participate in activities resolved this issue rather quickly.

Evaluation and Parental Rights

As a parent you have rights relating to the evaluation of your child. They are important. A comprehensive and individual evaluation is the first step in developing your child's IEP. The importance of the evaluation cannot be overstated. Indeed a federal district court has ruled that an IEP cannot be appropriate unless the underlying evaluation was complete. East. PA. School District v. Scott B, (1999).

You have the following rights; study them, know them, and use them as necessary.

Most important is your right to not have your child evaluated without your written consent. This will require a conference with school personnel, which will afford you the opportunity to ask questions. Although most parents are anxious to have an evaluation in order to obtain necessary educational services, the school cannot do one without your consent. This is consistent with the requirement of parental participation in all phases of the development and implementation of your child's IEP.

There are two parts to an evaluation. One is to determine whether your child is a "child with a disability," and the other is to aid the IEP team in determining appropriate educational needs. In other words, what is in the eligibility determination will form the basis for at least the first IEP you will develop.

It is important to remember that no services can be provided until the evaluation is complete.

The evaluation must include a review of all existing data. The evaluator must take into account any information that you choose to provide, including your observations and opinions, as well as medical records.

The evaluation must include information from you as to your opinion of your child's ability to participate in general education curriculum. The trend of law over the past generation has been toward the inclusion of children with disabilities in regular classrooms and away from placements in classrooms exclusively reserved for children with disabilities. I will discuss this in detail in the chapter on inclusion. But this is your first opportunity to put a school district on notice of your wishes regarding inclusion.

The evaluation must cover all areas of suspected disability. The evaluation determination will form your first present level of performance (PLOP) and be of great importance to the IEP team in determining your child's educational needs.

The law requires a comprehensive evaluation. It should address all of your child's needs, including needs not ordinarily associated with your child's condition. For example, a child with Down syndrome may also have mobility issues.

No single testing method or style may be used. The requirement of "comprehensive" requires that your child be evaluated in a manner most appropriate for her or him.

The district must assure that evaluation materials not be culturally or racially discriminatory.

If you are not satisfied with the evaluation you receive from the district you have the right to ask for an independent evaluation at school expense.

There are times when parents have felt that evaluators working for a school district may not comply with the requirements of the law. A common suspicion is a reluctance to find a child eligible in order to contain the costs associated with special education. For that reason you may request a qualified evaluator with no financial link to the district.

The school has the right to ask you why you disagree with the school's evaluation, but they cannot require you to answer.

Within a "reasonable time" of your request for an independent evaluation, the school must either agree to pay for it or take steps to convene a hearing to show why its evaluation is appropriate. This is one of those potentially nasty situations. If you feel that you are right and they are wrong, you should ask for an independent evaluation. I would simply caution you to pick your battles. A minimum precaution is to speak to your selected evaluator first, and find out specifically what they believe are the shortcomings of the school's evaluation.

Once your child has been determined eligible for special education services, there is a reevaluation called for every three years. Thanks to the amendments to IDEA in 1997, the school cannot force a reevaluation unless it has "reason to believe" that your child is no longer a "child with a disability." Reevaluations make sense because often an eligible child will make enough progress that special education services are no longer needed. But before the 1997 amendments there was a lot of time and money wasted on needless evaluations. For children with developmental disabilities, such as mental retardation, the disabling condition is not going to go away after three years of services.

Your consent is required before any reevaluation can be done. On the other hand, you may request a reevaluation at any time.

PART 3
Lesson #1:
The IEP Drives Your Services!

The IEP drives your services! What is written in your IEP is the basis for the school's delivery of educational services to your child. If the service is not in the IEP the school is under no obligation to provide it.

If services are in your IEP, and the school fails to provide them, there are procedures to force compliance. However, if you file a Complaint with your State Educational Authority (SEA) or decide on a Due Process Hearing and the service you claim the district failed to provide is not clearly spelled out in the IEP you will not be successful.

The most important single skill you need as a parent is the ability to participate meaningfully in the writing of a clear and measurable IEP for your child.

The law makes it clear that you are not a guest at the IEP meeting. You have a legally guaranteed right to be there. Always treat all members of your IEP team with respect but never forget that you are as important as anyone else.

It is so important for you to accept and appreciate your role in this process that it is worth taking a few lines to look at what the United States Supreme Court has said about it.

In the case of Honig v. Dole, 484 US 305, 311 (1998) the Court called the IEP the "centerpiece of the (IDEA's) education delivery system." The process of developing the IEP and the document itself are more than mere technicalities.

[Note on legal citations. This is not a law book. But parents do need to be able to decipher legal jargon. The citation above is consistent with others you will see and it means Volume 484 of a set of law books called the United States Reporter. The case cited begins on page 305 and the quotation is taken from page 311]

In addressing parent participation in IEP meetings, the Supreme Court in a case commonly referred to as Rowley, 458 US 176, said at page 204:

> *"It seems to us no exaggeration to say that Congress placed every bit as much emphasis upon compliance with procedures giving parents and guardians a large measure of participation at every stage of the administrative process... as it did upon the measurement of the resulting IEP against a substantive standard. We think that the Congressional emphasis upon full participation of concerned parties throughout the*

*development of the IEP…demonstrates the legislative
conviction that adequate compliance with the procedures
prescribed would in most cases assure much if not all of
what Congress wished in the way of substantive content in
the IEP."*

As I said, we parents are not guests.

Additional Parent Rights

Before an IEP meeting can take place, parents must be afforded certain rights. Not all of them apply to you in every situation, but you must know them and make sure they are being honored.

You have the right to a written notice of the time and place of the IEP meeting. This notice must be delivered to you a reasonable time before the proposed meeting.

Generally, meetings take place during normal working hours. Many school personnel are covered by union contracts, which prohibit evening or weekend meetings. If you cannot work out the time for the meeting, you have the right to participate by conference call.

Because the law requires cultural competency, parents have the right to request interpreters in their native language if needed.

In preparation for the meeting, schools must consider the results of evaluations, the strengths of the child, and the concerns of his or her parents in developing the IEP.

Parents are full-fledged members of the IEP team.

Parents must be given the opportunity to participate in every meeting regarding the identification, evaluation, educational placement, and provision of FAPE.

PART 4
What Is an IEP team?

An IEP can only be developed at a meeting, or meetings of the IEP team. The requirements for membership of an IEP team are set out in IDEA.

An IEP team must be composed of the following members:

- The parents of a child with a disability.
- At least one regular education teacher of that child (if the child is or may be participating in a regular education environment).
- At least one special education teacher, or, where appropriate, at least one provider of special education services (such as a physical therapist or speech pathologist) of the child.
- A representative of the school who
- Is qualified to provide, or supervise the provision of, specially designed instruction to meet the unique needs of children with disabilities.
- Is knowledgeable about the general curriculum.
- Is knowledgeable about the availability of resources of the local education agency (the school district).
- An individual who can interpret the instructional implications of evaluation results.
- At the discretion of the parent or the school, other individuals who have knowledge or special expertise regarding the child, including related services personnel.
- Whenever appropriate, the child with the disability.

A regular education teacher is involved with the team in order to help determine behavioral strategies, supplemental aids and services, program modifications and supports for school personnel. Depending on a student's needs and the purpose of the meeting, the regular education teacher is not required to attend the whole meeting or to attend all IEP meetings. Since the law leans strongly toward including children with disabilities in at least some portion of regular curriculum, the regular education teacher is included. An important consideration at the meeting is support and training for school personnel who will be expected to teach a child with a disability in their classroom. Not every teacher is trained in special education, but they are all expected to teach children with disabilities. This is only possible with technical support and training from the school district. Many a placement has failed because the IEP team did not clearly indicate the level of supports the classroom teacher would need.

It is good practice for schools and parents to reach agreement in advance on the parameters of the regular education teacher's participation. A good rule is to ask for the participation only in that portion of the IEP the regular education teacher will be asked to implement.

Schools are encouraged, and you should encourage it as well, to obtain input from any teachers who may not be attending the meeting.

The "district representative" is a key member of the IEP team. The first thing you should do when a meeting begins is to make sure you know exactly who that person is. Sometimes they will be a familiar face from within the school and often they are from a more central administrative agency.

A common clash between parents and school officials is in the interpretation of IDEA language (quoted above) as to whether or not the school representative must be someone with the authority to allocate school resources at the IEP meeting. Why this is a misunderstanding is curious. The IEP team is required to design both an educational plan and the strategies to implement that plan. That's what the meeting is about. Every IEP requires the allocation of district resources be it teacher time, an educational assistant, technical assistance produces and devices or modified curriculum. Those decisions need to be made on the spot or the meeting cannot conclude successfully.

It seems clear to me that the school representative must be someone with the authority to commit school resources and who can assure that the services set out in the IEP will actually be provided. This is a question you should settle before the meeting.

The IEP Content

You are now, finally, ready for your IEP meeting. Keep your head clear and keep your mind on the outcome. Remember what you know. You are a full-fledged member of the team. You have a valid evaluation. The team is assembled and you are remembering that the IEP drives your services! This is the meeting that will make the education plan for your child.

An IEP is a carefully written document. It must set out in detail the nature of your child's educational needs, the services that will be provided by the school and the goals specific to your child.

Every IEP is written on a preprinted form. The form contains all of the legally mandated requirements and space to fill in the details. For some reason there is no standardized form. The form you will use will probably be different from those in another state and in all probability are different from others within your own state. Before the meeting, ask to be provided with the official IEP form that will be used in your meeting. Study it and get familiar with it. Doing so will make the meeting go more smoothly and will mean there is one less unfamiliar thing that can upset your concentration.

The first thing an IEP must do is to list the child's present level of performance (PLOP.) This is your baseline to decide what to do next and will be used as a measurement of progress. The PLOP should indicate how your child's disability affects his or her involvement and participation in general curriculum.

The IEP must list annual goals and short-term objectives or benchmarks. You need to think ahead of time about just what it is you want your child to learn in the next year and make sure your wishes are written in one or more of the annual goals. (See Chapter 6 for details on goal writing.)

The goals must be measurable and they must relate to meeting your child's educational needs including those that will enable your child to be involved with and to make progress in the general curriculum.

The IEP must include all special education and related services and supplementary aids and services to be provided to your child, or on behalf of your child. If, for example, your goal is to have your child learn to do multiplication tables, you must specify precisely what that means. "Johnny will learn to multiply numbers up to five," is a goal. How will it be achieved? "Johnny will receive thirty minutes of math instruction three days a week from the special education math instructor."

What about the rest of the week? If Johnny is to receive instruction in a regular education classroom, how can the IEP help the teacher? "The classroom teacher will have two hours a term of consultation time with the special education math instructor to aid in continuing classroom instruction. The consultation will take place in the classroom, before school the first four Tuesdays of the term."

The IEP must also list all program modifications and supports for school personnel, that will help the child to:

- Attain the annual goals.
- Participate and progress in the general curriculum.
- Be educated with both disabled and non-disabled classmates.
- Participate in extracurricular and nonacademic activities.

This requirement is here to remind the team that regular education teachers need supports and training in order to include children with a wide variety of learning abilities, styles, and needs. If the classroom teacher needs help, that help, in terms of training or consultation, needs to be spelled out in the IEP.

Modifications continue to be an issue. A modification is a change in the regular curriculum that enables a child with a disability to participate in the class. People should make them with training in curriculum modification in consultation with classroom staff. This requires coordination with your special education office and must be detailed in the IEP if you expect it to happen.

The IEP must specify precisely when services are to begin as well as their frequency, location, and duration. This may seem tedious but it pays off. Typically IEPs happen in the spring and are directed at the following school year. Specify that services and modifications will begin on the first day of school. There is a sad history of IEP implementation where everything is ready for regular education students the first day of school, but the "special" arrangements are not. Your student is entitled to the same number of instructional days as everyone else. Be sure the dates are in the IEP.

Transition to Adult Life

The IEP must also include provisions to assist students in making the transition from school to adult living. These are called transition services. They are detailed in a separate chapter. But, beginning at age fourteen, the IEP must include the transition service needs related to the child's course of study. At age sixteen, or younger if appropriate, actual transition services are to begin. The IEP must list those services.

Regular Education, Standardized Tests and Assessments

Because the law favors students with disabilities participating in regular curriculum to whatever extent is appropriate, the IEP must spell out the extent to which your student will not participate with non-disabled classmates in academic and nonacademic settings. This is a big change in the educational paradigm. Instead of listing those rare occasions when children are educated in regular settings, it is now presumed that all education will take place with non-disabled classmates except for those times of the day specified in the IEP.

If your student is to participate in state or district wide assessments of student achievement (and, given the requirements of the Federal No Child Left Behind law, the pressure is on for them to do so) the IEP must specify any modifications that will be made in the actual tests. Modifications can include such things as extra time, having the test read to the student, recording answers in an alternative format, such as dictating into a recorder, using a computer, or dictating to another person. They may also include the use of a calculator, electronic spell checker, or other appropriate modifications.

Students with disabilities may not be required to participate in district and statewide assessments. If you choose for your child to not participate, the IEP must say so. If that is the case the IEP must specify some other method by which your student's performance will be assessed.

Measurements, Reviews, and Modifications

How will your child's progress toward the annual goals be measured? Those measurements must be included in the IEP. Progress reports must be provided to you in writing at least as often as traditional report cards go out to other parents.

An IEP is valid for one year and must be reviewed at least annually. This is true whether or not the goals have been achieved. The IEP can be revised as often as necessary, and the school or the parents may call an IEP review meeting at any time. The same rules concerning notification and team membership apply at any review meeting.

If there are behavioral concerns, the IEP must specify what the student's behavioral needs are and what interventions will occur.

Children with limited English proficiency have the right to have their needs met. Those accommodations must be listed in the IEP.

If the child is blind or visually impaired, the use of Braille or other strategy must be included in the IEP. The same is true of modifications of needs for students who are deaf or hard of hearing.

All assistive technology needed to make progress on the annual goals must be included in the IEP.

The final IEP must be made available to each regular education or special education teacher, as well as to other providers of services. It must be available to anyone responsible for any part of its implementation. Additionally, the school must inform every team member of their specific responsibilities, as well as the accommodations, modifications and supports the student will need.

Good, Bad and Ugly

I have attended at least two hundred IEP meetings. Some were for Eleanor and, obviously, others were in my capacity as advocate for parents. In all of these meetings, the same general principles of special education advocacy were used. Obviously the same law was applied. But outcomes vary dramatically.

Thinking about those experiences makes me wonder what lessons can be learned from a short review of some of them.

Good

Most of Eleanor's IEP meetings have been relatively pleasant, and all have been successful. In thinking about why this is true, I return again and again to thorough preparation. It is also helpful to have your child attend as early in his or her life as possible. Even when they are too small to make a contribution it is a good idea to have them there is only for a few moments. It reminds the team of just whom they are dealing with. Meetings are not for parents and school people to hassle each other. They are to create a meaningful educational program.

When Eleanor was in second grade we had a huge IEP meeting. We brought four or five people with us and the district had at least ten. There was a lot of tension and the stakes were high. The meeting took place before school, which made it convenient to have Eleanor come in before beginning class. She came in looking very solemn and uncomfortable. The school people's demeanor changed immediately and they began smiling and greeting her. She said nothing and showed no particular emotion. I took her hand to walk out of the room when one of the school people said, "She is such a happy girl." Eleanor stood up straight, and said in her most emphatic tone, "I am not happy!" Her statement made her very human and her presence continued to be felt throughout the meeting.

The lesson here is to keep your child front and center. Do everything possible to remind people of why you are there, and move heaven and earth to avoid its becoming a test of wills between your personality and those of school people.

Another year, a meeting was attended by school personnel who all knew Eleanor well and supported our desire for an inclusion placement the following year. The district representative, on the other hand, was a stranger to us all. The only thing he knew about her was what was in his file.

The meeting went along fine. Those of us who knew the situation were making good progress, while the district representative actually fell asleep. He awakened with a jerk, cleared his throat and said, "Shouldn't we review *his* placement options."

We all looked and him and the school principal said, "No." He went back to his nap. Later he shook himself awake again and said, "Is *he* getting the most benefit from this placement?"

The team all looked embarrassed and shocked. I said to him, "Mr. So and So, are you absolutely sure you are at the right IEP? Twice you have spoken up to change her placement and you have changed her sex." Everyone laughed, even him.

The lesson here is that humor can get you by better than conflict. The other point is that we had such a good relationship with the school staff that they were "on our side" when it came to the boorish district representative. That was where respect, listening, some kind words, a small holiday gift, etc., paid off handsomely.

Bad

The worst IEP we ever had for Eleanor was her first one. She had finished pre-school and was transitioning to kindergarten. We were very anxious that she attend our neighborhood school with her kid friends from the block. We were also unfamiliar with the new procedures and personalities. The school was making serious suggestions that she be bussed to a self-contained classroom several miles away.

In an attempt to work this all out we invited the district representative to come to Eleanor's mom's law office for an informal discussion. I think the legal setting must have intimidated the district representative more than we knew, because in no time we had worked out all of the details, shook hands, and she was on her way. We thought it was a big success.

However, when the first meeting was scheduled she acted like our other meeting had not happened. She denied making any agreements and was very distant and hostile, and the more she behaved that way the madder we got. The meeting ended with a lot of acrimony and a new one was scheduled.

We felt so ambushed, lied to, and misled that our anger just got more acute. Finally we made a serious decision that I would not recommend. We decided not to attend the next meeting at all. Instead, we wrote our desires out in a letter and sent our poor county case manager to the meeting to read it to the team. Basically it said that meeting with them was a waste of time, we had been lied to and misled, and they could do whatever they wished but we would not dignify their charade by attending.

Surprisingly, the letter worked like a charm. They acted all hurt and sorry and, much to our amazement, the IEP they mailed us contained everything we asked for.

The lesson here is that inexperience can hurt you and when it does you must step back and do what your instinct tells you. Being in a confined space with that district representative was not going to be a positive experience for any of us. At least we knew that much. The distrust and anger were simply too high.

Looking back I am now also of the opinion that the district representative had simply gotten carried away at the informal meeting and said and done things that exceeded her authority. Rather than admit that to her colleagues, and to us, she decided to pretend it didn't happen and essentially accuse us of making it all up. It was just one of those times when things didn't work. We did what we did; the result was fine and time passed and bad feelings abated. You will do lots of IEP meetings. Get through them. Sometimes things work and sometimes they don't. If it is possible to avoid inexperienced parents working with an inexperienced and insecure district representative, that would be a good idea too.

I am certain that if we had been working with a more seasoned professional, none of this would have happened.

On another occasion I attended an early morning meeting on behalf of a sweet girl a few years younger than Eleanor. Her mom and dad are wonderful parents and have high hopes for their daughter. Their daughter is probably more difficult for the school to include than Eleanor is. But that is mostly an issue of shyness. The child in question is a perfectly functional, well meaning, high spirited little girl with plenty of learning potential.

But the school was crowded, the class chaotic, the teacher frazzled and the whole placement was going bad. When we arrived the district representative handed us a written agenda of how the meeting was to be handled. It was early in the morning, and the parents were anxious to get along with the school and continue their child's placement. We read over the agenda and, stupidly, agreed to it.

First of all, it limited the time for the whole meeting to forty minutes. The parents were limited to commenting during the final five minutes. The rest of the time was to be taken up with present level of performance, failures, the reason for a more restrictive placement, etc. About five minutes into this the parents got really anxious and increasingly frustrated with the feeling that they were bring shut out. I felt stupid for every agreeing to the agenda in the first place.

The meeting concluded with the team deciding on a new placement over the parent's objections. The parents felt so humiliated by the experience that they simply withdrew their daughter from school and home schooled her for a year.

The district bears a lot of responsibility for this. Their training should clearly have let people know that a written agenda, which limits parent participation, is unacceptable. We should have known better than to agree to such a suggestion. The lesson is that these procedural rules and safeguards are there for a reason. Use them.

Ugly

It seems impossible that parents would behave the way I describe below. Unfortunately they do. Be sure, as your last thought before starting a meeting, that you are thinking about what is best for your child. IEP meetings are a place for discipline.

These two IEP meetings stand out in my mind as absolute nightmares. One more than the other although they have similarities. And the similarity has to do with adult relationships that are on the rocks and feuding parents, barely speaking to one another, showing up with no common strategy or agreement to act together for the benefit of their child. The meeting became just another place for them to bring their personal dispute. In both cases a husband or a lover, who knew next to nothing about special education, hampered the mother's effort. The moms and their now former partners could not resist the temptation to insult and ridicule one another. I can't imagine a more toxic blend.

Far and away the worst one involved a high school boy with autism and an assortment of neurological disabilities. His functioning is very limited. There was no question that he would continue in a combination life-skills and behavioral classroom. The child had a lot of bad behavior and is large and rather intimidating when angry. Mom did not want to admit that and insisted that all the problems had to do with the arrogant incompetence of the school people. Good advocates do not expect the school to "fix" their child. They accept reality and work toward the best program. No one on the school side of this IEP was responsible for her child's disability or bad behavior.

What made this even odder is that the mom is a professional advocate and presumptive leader in the special education community. She has a powerful and assertive personality that had carried her a long way in the state legislature, etc. She is very used to throwing her political weight around and having people obey her every command. While her appetite for the sound of her own voice appears boundless, she loses interest quickly at the sound of others'.

By the time I was asked to attend, there had been several very hostile meetings, and a facilitator had been hired. The tension in the room was so great that the district people spoke only to the facilitator. No one could speak directly to one another although we were ten feet apart. The district's side of the table featured a partner from one of Portland's largest law firms brought in at great expense to support their position that trying to set a self-help goal of teaching the student to make a sandwich was unrealistic! It was a mess!

The mother's behavior got more and more bizarre with threats of a due process hearing, talking to legislators about education funding, and just a sense of total, blind, and irrational rage. After a while we took a break and some of this dysfunctional behavior came into focus.

Her estranged husband was there, of course. I had not realized the extent of their anger with one another. During the break, they hurled

105

insults back and forth, stomped around, kicked the wall, and generally behaved in all the ways that this community leader has asserted to parents in her trainings that no one should ever behave. I was totally embarrassed to be there.

The result of the IEP was terrible. No one who was there felt well about how ugly and unproductive it was. It even involved the end of the mom's friendship with the special education director. It mixed up public and private issues. And, above all, it illustrated that adult relationships and their demise have no place at an IEP meeting.

Only at the meeting had I realized that the parents had not talked ahead of time; the mother behaved as if the father was an infantile fool whose opinion was worse than the schools. He, naturally, got, all-defensive, and basically they acted out their end-of-marriage melodrama as if it were some kind of Passion Play for all to see. No one, but them, had any interest in that subject. It made them both look absurd and did nothing to help their child.

This is not the only IEP I have gotten myself into without realizing that I was in the middle of a relationship break-up where anger and jealousy were the motivating forces. If you are going through something like this, all I can say is think about your child. Maybe it is best if only one parent attend. Maybe it is best if neither of them do. I do know that this was the worst excuse for an IEP meeting that I have ever witnessed. I still don't know why I was invited since the mom's rage was such she would allow no one but herself to speak. It certainly has left me wondering why Congress went to so much trouble to provide a forum to be used so inappropriately.

Keep your personal life personal. Don't bring it to the IEP meeting.

I have attended meetings that lasted up to twenty hours over many days. Obviously these are the exception and show a lack of good preparation and communication. But even the longest of these was obviously a heartfelt attempt by parents to do what was right for their child and to express some hope for more sensitivity and skill-building among professionals. They ended as successes.

Be humble, prepared, and assertive all at the same time. Keep your eye on the prize.

This is not a place to come in and throw your weight around from another arena of your life. Focus on what is in front of you. It is your child that matters. You have plenty of places in your life to show off.

Remember your child.

Notes on a Name

The current, correct name for the law we are dealing with is the Individuals with Disabilities Education Improvement Act of 2004. The acronym **is IDEIA.** Throughout the book I have mostly used the old name, the Individuals with Disabilities Education Act and the old acronym **IDEA.**

One of the reasons for this is simply familiarity and comfort. But the new law, IDEIA, is, in fact, the first time since 1974 that Congress backtracked on the rights of children and families.

Reduced Attorney fee schemes for Due Process Hearings, details of discipline, the federal contribution, and strengthening the hand of schools and administrators is the legacy of these amendments.

Knuckling under and accepting the additional insult of labeling this law an "improvement" act is something most of us cannot do without gagging. You may call it what you want. The fact is that Congress did us no favors in the reenactment.

To add insult to injury, President Bush's 2006-2007 budget, now submitted and pending in Congress, recommends a further *reduction* in the federal contribution to the cost of special education. Far from honoring the original Congressional promise of full funding for special education, the administration is running away from it as fast as possible.

Chapter 4

OTHER IDEA SERVICES

*"Arriving at one goal is the starting point
for another."*

John Dewey

Extended School Year
Assistive Technology
Transition Services
Positive Behavioral Support
Section 504

Students are entitled to a menu of other IDEA services. Each is designed to meet the educational needs of the child with a goal of promoting independence, educational success and equal opportunity.

Extended School Year (ESY)

All advocacies for students in special education are built on the same bedrock principles. Some students with disabilities require a longer than usual school year in order to receive a Free and Adequate Public Education (FAPE). That is the same principle underlying IEP meetings, related services, etc.

A standard school year calendar is not necessarily the outer limit on the legal entitlement to an appropriate education. Your argument is this, "In order for my child's education to be *adequate* he or she is entitled to a longer instructional year."

ESY Is Not Summer School

Naturally there are some definitions and rules relating to ESY that complicates it and turns it into something with a meaning quite different from what one might think from just reading the words. The first thing to know about ESY is that it is not summer school.

Summer school is not something that school districts are required to offer. If they do offer it, students are free to choose to participate or not.

ESY, on the other hand, is available to children with disabilities because the child needs to participate in order to attain a FAPE. Because of the child's need for ESY services the district cannot, under any circumstances, charge tuition. ESY services are part of the "free and appropriate public education" the school district is obligated to provide.

Because ESY is part of a child's FAPE the services must be tailored to meet the child's individualized needs, as set out in the IEP. It is not appropriate to put a child into an existing summer school program and pretend it is ESY when the child's IEP reflects individual requirements different from what is offered in the summer school program.

ESY Eligibility

It is unavoidable to use some very technical and legal sounding terms in describing the eligibility tests of ESY. The two to pay most attention to are "substantial regression" and "recouped."

The question is whether a child will or can be expected to experience substantial regression during the summer months when there is no instructional program and whether the skills lost could not be recouped within a reasonable period of time after school begins in the fall.

The problem with this test is that it is easier to state than to implement. One thing we know for sure is that districts cannot categorically deny special education students an ESY and that the test must be one based on individual need.

School districts must adopt procedures for ESY that comply with federal and state law. Even though these procedures comply with the law, they may vary greatly in their detail and local requirements. The first thing you should do is to ask your district for a copy of their ESY rules and procedures.

There are enough similarities, however, for us to look at common themes and develop a plan to obtain ESY services when appropriate. Local plans generally have these two things in common with one another. To be eligible, the child must be: 1) Eligible for special education and be a person for whom maintenance of their level of self-sufficiency and independence is unlikely, after an interruption of services, in view of their disabling conditions, without ESY services; or 2) students eligible for special education who require an ESY in order to remain in their current least restrictive environment (LRE) placement.

"Self-sufficiency" skills are skills or areas of learning that lead to independence. These can be things necessary for basic independence or for community living.

Basic independence includes the skills necessary to maintain independent toileting, control of muscles, feeding and eating independently, dressing and hygiene, mobility and academics. Community living skills include behavior control, interpersonal relationships, personal hygiene, communication, etc. as shown by interacting with other students, faculty, staff, and adults.

What Is an ESY Decision Based On?

The IEP team decides ESY eligibility based upon sources of information that may be used to determine a child's likelihood to regress, i.e., to lose skills they currently have, along with the child's capacity to relearn those skills in a reasonable time after school begins again in the fall.

You need to learn these sources of information and proactively keep written records of your own and encourage your child's teachers and related services staff to do so as well. The main time, obviously, is the lengthy vacation around the Christmas holiday. Look closely at how your child is doing before and after that break. This is part of the basic skill of documentation that every successful family advocate must make develop.

Additionally, look at progress on goals on consecutive IEPs. How has your child's present level of performance (PLOP) been impacted by interruptions in the instructional year?

Obtain, keep, and refer to progress reports done by teachers, related services staff such as therapists, and others who have direct contact with the child. Pay particular attention to how these reports reflect changes in PLOP before and after interruptions.

Your own observations are crucial and of the most importance. You have more direct contact with your child than anyone. Write down and keep your contemporary observations about negative changes in behaviors and life skills before and after break periods. Be sure to keep watching to see how long it takes your child to get back to where they were before the break. Those observations are relative to a team's determination of what a "reasonable" period of time is for skills to be "recouped."

Another category of people who have direct contact with your child is physicians and health care workers. Check their reports to see if they reflect degenerative difficulties which become more acute during breaks in educational services.

Observations by others at the school as well as family members, community members, clergy, music teachers, etc., are always relevant. You don't have to have a college degree in order to have an opinion.

Results of any testing done just before and just after a break can also be reflective of the need for ESY.

Another way of stating this, another way of looking at the issue is to ask the team whether, in the absence of ESY services, the child is likely to require catch-up or compensatory services in the fall. Will the child have to move to a more restrictive educational placement because of lost independence and social skills? Will the child become less independent in daily life skills? Will the child, if living outside the family home, require moving to a less independent living arrangement? Will the child be less able to obtain job training and employment?

Remember that the details of these tests vary from state to state and from district to district. Get a written copy of the procedures followed by your school. Apply the tests, criteria, and suggestions outlined above.

How Do We Get ESY Services?

Most parents, and many educators, agree with me that it is an oddity that districts have no obligation to bring up ESY at meetings. ESY must be considered at the child's IEP meeting only if the parents, or the school district, bring it up. Be prepared at the IEP meeting to provide any relevant observations, notes or data supporting ESY for your child.

If, for some reason, ESY services become an issue after your IEP you can request in writing to your district's Director of Special

Education that your child be evaluated for ESY services. The district must then convene the IEP Team to consider ESY services.

Procedural Protections

If you are denied ESY services you may assert your rights under IDEA and probably Section 504. These protections are the same ones you assert any time there is a disagreement about FAPE. You can ask for mediation, go to a due process hearing, obtain written findings, and appeal to state or federal court.

These are extreme remedies and most families avoid them by careful documentation and advocacy.

Some Personal Experiences

Our daughter received ESY services for several years. They were appropriate at the time and were very helpful. When we no longer needed them we thanked the district for what they had done and no longer asked for them.

They were helpful to her because we had chosen for her what is commonly called an "inclusion" model. We wanted her to learn to live, interact, learn from and enjoy the neighborhood children she lives around whether or not they had a disability.

Because of her developmental delays, size, and general timidity she had a hard time getting back to a successful comfort level with her classmates after a period of school interruption. This didn't have much to do with PLOP, but it had a lot to do with a danger that her educational placement could change to a more restrictive environment. We documented her behaviors and asked others to do so as well. Based on those observations, we obtained ESY services.

Once you are going to get them, what do they look like? In our case we wanted her to have enough structured interaction with kids over the summer to avoid an "unreasonable" amount of time to "recoup" her skills when school ended. We did that by looking at Park and Recreation Programs, day camps, little outings and events. We brought the details of those things to the IEP meeting along with our arguments about why they were necessary. The result was that the school district agreed to pay for anywhere from two to four weeks of fun activity for her over the summer. Note the personal nature of the request. We came in with a plan for what would benefit this one child and her unique needs. The results were spectacular.

This is one area of advocacy where your creativity can pay off. Come to the meeting with a reading program you like or other ideas. It is easier for schools to pay a small amount of money for your child to participate in a necessary summer activity than it is to set up their own program and hire staff.

Remember that ESY is not summer school. Districts, feeling beleaguered, may try to sell you on some kind of one-size-fits-all summer school for the disabled. That is an administrative convenience. It is not ESY.

Assistive Technology (AT)

IDEA requires schools to ensure that eligible children with disabilities receive a FAPE that includes special education, related services, and supplemental aids and services without charge to the parent and in conformity with the IEP. Once again our advocacy returns to a foundation constructed with our old friend FAPE. Your child will receive Assistive Technology as a supplemental aid if it is required by FAPE. Your advocacy strategy must focus on "appropriate." If the service is found by the IEP team to be one required in order to provide a FAPE then it must be included in the IEP.

What Is Assistive Technology?

The short answer is that any gadget designed or modified to help your child achieve the goals and objectives of her/his IEP is assistive technology. Assistive technology includes any equipment or device that make it easier for someone who has a disability to maintain or increase functioning in a life activity. Examples include wheelchairs, communication devices, adapted hand controls, modifications, etc. Things as simple as pens and pencils are AT as well as adapted toys.

Naturally the more formal definitions sound wordier.

"Any item, piece of equipment, or product system, whether acquired commercially off the shelf, modified, or customized, that is used to increase, maintain, or improve the functional capabilities of children with disabilities," is an assistive technology device.

"Any service that directly assists a child with a disability in the selection, acquisition, or use of an assistive technology device," is an assistive technology service. Those services include:

The evaluation of the needs of a child with a disability, including a functional evaluation of the child in the child's customary environment;

Purchasing, leasing, or otherwise providing for the acquisition of assistive technology services by children with disabilities;

Selecting, designing, fitting, customizing, adapting, applying, retaining, repairing, or replacing assistive technology services or device;

Coordinating and using other therapies, interventions, or services with assistive technology devices, such as those associated with existing education and rehabilitation plans and programs;

Training or technical assistance for a child with a disability, or if appropriate, that child's family; and

Training or technical assistance for professionals (including individuals providing education or rehabilitation services), employers, or other individuals who provide services to, employ, or are otherwise substantially involved in the major life functions of children with disabilities.

Under the law, assistive technology is only required when it is educationally "relevant." It will only be provided if its need is established by the IEP process to be (1) special education; (2) a related service; or (3) a supplementary aid or service required to enable a child to be educated in the least restrictive environment.

However you state it, the advocacy plan to obtain it continues to focus on FAPE. If circumstances are such that assistive technology devices and/or services are necessary to achieve a FAPE, then they must be provided.

A determination whether an assistive technology device or service is required in order for a child to receive a FAPE must be made on an individual basis using the local district's existing procedures for evaluation, development of the IEP, and placement.

Evaluation

Individual evaluation is a concept central to IDEA. If a district, or any educational agency involved with the child, suspects that the child may need assistive technology devices and/or services in order to receive a FAPE, a child's evaluation must include an assessment of his or her need for assistive technology devices and services. Parents can request such an assessment at any time. All of the procedural protections related to evaluations in other parts of IDEA apply to assistive technology assessments. Like all evaluations, people who are qualified to make them must do the evaluation. In cases where school or agency personnel do not have the knowledge to provide assistive technology services, public funds may be used to obtain the necessary expertise, and, if appropriate, training for educational staff.

The Role of the IEP

The IEP team that, of course, must take into account the needs of the individual child must determine the need for assistive technology. If the team determines that a child requires assistive technology or services in order to receive a FAPE, the IEP must include a specific statement of such services, including the nature and amount of those services. It is not sufficient to find that AT services are needed. They must be spelled out in detail as part of the IEP. The detail must include a specific description of the device or services, who is responsible for obtaining those things, a deadline to obtain them, how often they will be used, who will repair them, where will they be kept, etc. The IEP team can also determine whether a FAPE requires home use of the devices or services.

If home use is determined to be required, the IEP must set out the circumstances of home use including how the device will be transported to and from school, set-up and home repair, and the needs of the family to be trained in its use.

If the device is a communication board or a computer, the need for training family members will, clearly, be more acute than if the AT is a modified can opener. Decisions vary from person to person. The one thing they have in common is the requirement that they be focused on one individual at a time.

Placement

Assistive technology and services are intended to help carry out IDEA's mandate that children with disabilities will be educated in the least restrictive environment. Separate schooling, special classes out of the ordinary curriculum or other removal of children with disabilities from the regular educational environment cannot happen unless the IEP team finds that the nature and severity of the child's disability is such that education in a regular classroom with the use of supplemental aids and services cannot be satisfactorily achieved.

There can be no such thing as an assistive technology "ghetto" for special education kids. The services and devices are intended to promote placement in the least restrictive environment. The point of assistive technology is to allow greater independence and productivity.

Payment for Devices and Services

If the IEP team determines that assistive technology devices and services are required for a FAPE, then they must be provided at no cost to the family of the child with a disability. That seems simple but can be complicated by private insurance. Many families have insurance to pay for durable medical goods such as communication devices, mobility devices, etc.

Schools cannot require a family to use their private insurance coverage to pay for assistive technology called for in an IEP. On the other hand there is no prohibition against it either. The use of insurance is voluntary. Families need to be careful about volunteering to use private insurance. Particular attention should be paid to whether or not such use will unnecessarily reduce available lifetime coverage.

Special education funds may be used to pay for evaluations, the purchase or lease of the assistive technology, training and technical assistance for its use including, where appropriate, training family members. The funds may also be used for training and technical assistance for teachers, staff, employers, or other individuals who provide services, etc.

There are sources to pay for AT other than schools. If your child is Medicaid eligible there are funding possibilities. There are categories of AT called "durable medical equipment" (DME) that can now be paid for by Medicaid. DME basically covers an item that you can use for a long time that meets a medical need. Federal law now requires private insurance carriers to follow federal Medicaid rules in defining assistive technology.

Recourse

If the school determines that assistive technology is not necessary for the provision of FAPE, but the parents believe that it is, the parent has procedural recourse that varies in its detail from one agency to another. Generally the recourse includes a complaint to the state educational agency, mediation, and a due process hearing. Obtain the written procedures maintained by your school.

Standards for Determining the Need for AT

Is it special education or a related service?

If a student is using a computer with the goal of learning, the use of assistive technology is special education. If another student is using a computer in order to gain access to educational benefit, then, that assistive technology is a related service. It is important to know where to place the service requirement within the IEP.

Assistive Technology as Special Education

A rub in special education is that schools are not required under IDEA to provide educational opportunity that maximizes a student's potential. They are required only to provide services that are an educational benefit. In other words, parents want a Cadillac program, but schools are only required to provide a bus. Nowhere is this clearer than in the area of assistive technology. All of our kids' educational potential may be maximized by the use of every gadget and gizmo.

But schools need only provide services that make it likely the student will receive benefit.

Furthermore, some courts have set the standard so low that schools have not been required to provide assistive technology if the benefit to the child is so little or so speculative that it is not deemed necessary for a FAPE. But, even if you are denied assistive technology as part of special education on your IEP, you may succeed in getting it as a related service.

Assistive Technology as a Related Service

Related services must be provided to a child with a disability if the related services are found to "assist" the child to benefit from special education. Thus, the question to be asked is, "Will the child benefit from special education if he or she receives a related service?" When this question is posed this way, rather than as a special education issue, it is more likely the school will agree to provide it.

Even if the special education benefit is so small and speculative as to not be part of FAPE, the assistive technology may be found to assist to benefit the child as a related service.

Medical services are not required to be provided as a related service unless they are necessary for evaluation or diagnostic services. A mental evaluation may be provided as a related service but a trip to the dentist will not.

Assistive Technology as a Supplementary Aid or Service

Assistive technology may be required as a supplemental aid or service if it is necessary to aid the student in participating in school in the least restrictive educational environment. The IEP team must consider whether assistive technology will allow a child to receive his or her FAPE in a more integrated setting.

In determining the placement of a child in a least restrictive environment the IEP team uses a balancing test, which is weighted, toward the least restrictive placement.

The factors included in that balancing test include:

- The benefit to the child with the disability;
- The benefits to the other students in the classroom from interacting with a student with a disability;

- The degree to which the curriculum must be modified by the teacher to accommodate the student with the disability; and
- The overall disruption to the regular classroom environment.

I suggest that you should use a similar balancing test while advocating for assistive technology as a supplementary aid or service.

A useful question to ask the IEP team is, "whether the conclusion derived from balancing these factors would be different if the student were provided with assistive technology in the more inclusive setting?" If the use of assistive technology makes possible the more inclusive setting, the assistive technology must be provided as a supplementary aid or service, and the student must be placed in that setting.

A Sample of AT Success Stories

Heartland Area Education Agency is located in Johnston, Iowa and provides services to 65,000 students. Some of the success stories they report can be used by you in advocating for AT for your child as well as placements in least restrictive environments.

A first grade teacher reported: "This technology has provided a way for him to stay included all day in the general education classroom."

A third grade teacher who uses the voice output communication device to "teach" a peer during class activity.

A junior high student who uses his communication board to negotiate with his teacher about how much homework can be assigned.

High school students use AT to present oral reports in science class.

The use of email can be a great help to teenagers working from a computer keyboard. (Don't forget those socialization goals.)

Keep in mind that by using AT a student will be able to:

- Read the same stories their peers will read.
- Write stories about their experiences and observations.
- Participate in more activities in the general education classrooms.
- Support reading and study skills, read at their own pace, reread passages, insert verbal notes, and access study skills supports.

Comment from a principal in Iowa.

"Technology has been so useful for our students with special needs, our general education teachers need to know about it. There is great application for our students in general education to access curriculum materials using some of the assistive technology strategies we have learned."

Comment from a teacher in Iowa.

"Following creation of a expanded keyboard setup which allows a student access to multiple displays for sentence writing – 'This student is so excited that he has twice as many words to write with! We have tried many ways to get computer access working for him and this is a real success.'"

The Assistive Technology Act

In 1988 Congress passed the Technology-Related Assistance for People with Disabilities Act (the "Tech Act"). It was reauthorized in September 2004. The purpose of the law is to provide information, technical assistance, and funding strategies. Each state, the District of Columbia and the Trust Territories have a federally funded

Technology Training and Information Center. These Centers have different names in each state. You can find yours on the Internet or by using a state services directory. Your center will provide you technical assistance in deciding what to purchase. Many of them will also do an assessment to investigate your child's AT needs.

Often people are unsure of what to use, how to use it, or where to buy it.

"Centers were created to assure that people with disabilities will be able to secure and effectively use assistive technology," says Lori Brooks, who heads the one in Oregon. "Centers are here to assure that a person gets the correct device."

Find and use the AT Information Center in your state. Use what you learn to propose AT in your IEP. They are a great source of information for IEP advocacy.

Transition Services

There comes a time in every students life where they transition out of school and into the adult world. Not every high school student successfully makes that transition. For children with disabilities this transition can be especially difficult. A disproportionate number of children with disabilities simply drop out of high school rather than face the uncertainty of adult life. Sometimes this behavior is simply a reflection of their family's desire to keep people with disabilities as perpetual children.

Being an adult with a disability is a challenge. But it is easier than it once was. Thanks to a US Supreme Court decision, commonly called *The Olmstead Case*, people with disabilities now have the right to chose to live in the community and not an institution or nursing home. More and more states are adopting adult service programs characterized as self-determination. Job supports, independent living, training in the use of assistive technology, the promotion of healthy intimate relationships, and respect and dignity are all within reach of Americans with disabilities today. The first step on the journey to independent living is high school transition.

The amendments to IDEA adopted in 2004 require IEP teams to begin the consideration of transition needs of students beginning not later than the first IEP in effect when the student is 16. Transition goals and planning must be a part of the student's IEP during each subsequent annual review. Transition services become an integral part of IEP and are designed to meet the unique needs of each student. The goal of transition services is to prepare the student for further education, employment, and independent living.

Student Participation in Transition Planning

Beginning with the IEP in effect when the student is sixteen the IEP team is required to invite the student to personally participate in the meeting. This is a major change in the composition of the team. Furthermore, the other team members must "actively involve" the student in the development of his/her IEP. For students, this can be a big adjustment in itself.

This new circumstance is recognition by IDEA of coming adulthood and the need for students with disabilities to receive exposure to a world where they will be called upon to make important decisions like any other adult. It is important to remember that the old model of people with disabilities as helpless victims who need perpetual protection from reality is over. As the expectation of an independent and dignified life has become the model, so too has the expectation that the person will take more responsibility for his or her own success and happiness.

This can be pretty scary for parents. Just remember all the bad decisions you have made. Don't deny your child with a disability the same opportunity. Professionals call this "the dignity of risk." With proper supports people with disabilities can make their wishes known. And they have the right to expect to be listened to.

Transfer of Rights

Whether parents like it or not a child with a disability is considered an adult when he or she turns 18. All procedural safeguards associated with IDEA transfer to the student at 18. Parents can attend IEP meetings if asked by their child. But it is now the child who makes the decisions and signs the forms.

The IEP team must plan ahead, and assist the student and parent in preparing and understanding for the transfer of rights that will occur. There are two time related events associated with transfer of rights.

At least one year before the student turns 18: On the IEP form, the team must document that discussions with the student regarding transfer of rights has occurred.

When the student reaches 18: The district must provide written notice of the transfer of rights to both the student and the parents. This written notice must be provided at the time of the student's birthday and not at the time of the annual review.

This event can come as quite a traumatic experience for parents who have been protecting and advocating for their child with a disability since birth. It does not mean that you are out of their lives. But you have to learn to live with some new circumstances.

Guardianship means that, in accordance with the vagaries of state laws, a judge has made a finding that a person is not competent to make his or her own important decisions. In the past, guardianship was commonly abused by simply assuming that everyone with a disability was incompetent. Modern practice has discredited that notion. However, guardianship is a viable alternative for families who feel that their child's disability is such as to make a mockery of notions like competence and decision-making. If you feel that guardianship is appropriate for your family member, you should speak to a lawyer in your state about its pros and cons. Remember, if you become your child's guardian you are responsible for making decisions during his or her adult years just like you did when he or she were infants.

Medicaid Eligibility

Medicaid is simply a cost-sharing plan between states and the federal government. Medicaid funds play a large role in financing the lives of people with disabilities who are unable to live independently on their own earned income or their family's assets. In order to qualify for Medicaid, the recipient must have personal assets, which are at or near the federal poverty level.

Until your child turns eighteen it is your family income that determines Medicaid eligibility. But once the child is eighteen it is only their personal assets that are counted. As a result nearly every child with any kind of significant disability becomes eligible for Medicaid benefits when they turn eighteen.

The nuances of Medicaid law are complex in the extreme. But what you need to know now is that the funds that become available to your child due to their new Medicaid eligibility can be used to fund some critical and creative transition plans. Pay particular attention to the next section on agency participation. From now on, you will have to deal with more public agencies than just the school district.

Benefits Planning

When a child with a disability reaches eighteen they may be eligible for benefits from Social Security or other agencies. School personnel are typically not aware of these benefits and often do not consider them to be within the scope of their responsibility.

If your child is receiving benefits such as Supplemental Security Income (SSI) or Title II Childhood Disability Benefits (CDB) they may require new eligibility standards at age 18. If you are not receiving any benefits you may find that your child is now eligible. Since school personnel seldom if ever receive training on Social Security and work incentives they are not, ordinarily, a good resource for this referral. Call the Social Security Office when your child nears his or her eighteenth birthday.

But these benefits serve as a valuable resource to eligible students as they transition from school to adult life. These benefit programs offer not only cash payments and health insurance, but also include numerous work incentives specifically designed to increase employment and earnings during and after transition from high school.

Failure to focus on these benefits during transition is a missed opportunity.

Ask your district representative about including these benefits, such as what is called a PASS Plan, into your transition plan. If the school is unable to help, check with your Social Security office.

Obviously, a transition plan is greatly improved with more resources. This is not a simple subject and its detail is beyond the scope of our discussion. But educating yourself on this issue is no different than any other. (See Appendix for resources on benefits planning.)

Agency Participation

Whenever transition issues are to be discussed at an IEP meeting, the school must invite a representative of any other agency likely to be responsible for providing or paying for transition services. If the agency does not attend, the IEP team must document their input.

Examples of other agency participation include your local office of Vocational Rehabilitation, community colleges, mental health services, developmental disabilities service office, your local independent living center, non-profit agencies, and service brokerages.

The transition plan you will help to create for your child will address broader goals and objectives than what you have been used to. It will require some new skills. For sure, it will require a lot of interagency coordination. That is never an easy task for anyone. Your school district will have staff familiar with various agencies that provide services. Get to know those staff people before the IEP meeting and stay in close contact with them. They are the people who will make the transition plan happen.

If a participating agency fails to carry out their responsibilities the school must, as soon as possible, initiate a meeting in order to find an alternative strategy in order to meet the IEP transition goals.

Post Secondary Goals and Transition Services

The main change in IEP goal writing is that your IEP must now contain appropriate measurable goals based upon age appropriate plans relating to training, education, employment and independent living skills. The IEP must include the services the student will require in order to meet his/her goals.

The course of study developed by the IEP team must relate directly to the adopted goals. Examples of a course of study based on independent living goals may include functional math, woodworking, training in the use of public transportation, community based work-experience, financial management, anger control, food preparation and management, shopping, living alone or sharing an apartment, etc.

This IEP addition is called the Course of Study Statement. It must address the classes, activities, and experiences the team has determined to be meaningful to the student's future, motivate the student to complete their studies and support adult outcomes. This statement can focus on academic classes if the team finds those to be realistic or it can focus on life-skills or vocational education and work experience.

Students eligible for services under IDEA can continue to receive them until the end of the school year following their 21st birthday. Since transition-planning must began at age 16, the transition services should be designed as part of a long-range plan. The plan should coordinate the last years of high school and the years that follow. The plan must focus on how best to facilitate movement from school to post-school activity.

In developing your plan, be sure to think about things such as vocational education, community integration and experiences, supported employment, independent living, independent mobility, continuing education, relationship building, etc.

Summary of Performance

The last IDEA service provided to students with a disability is called a Summary of Performance. It is provided to all students graduating with a regular high school diploma or leaving due to exceeding the age of eligibility. The Summary of Performance includes a summary of academic achievement and functional performance, and specific recommendations on how to help students meet their adult goals. These summaries are not required by IDEA 2004 but are provided in many states and are certainly a best practice. If your state does not do them as a matter of course, try to get something as close as possible.

Positive Behavior Support

There are lots of reasons why children with disabilities exhibit "behaviors." Some disabilities, such as emotional disturbances, attention deficit, autism, mental health issues, etc., simply include behavior that may be considered disruptive. In other situations children with disabilities, not unlike other children, will display bad behavior as a way to get attention, as a reaction to being ignored or isolated or, in not a small number of situations, just for fun.

A child who disrupts the educational opportunity of other children will wear out their welcome in a hurry. For children without disabilities the usual intervention is a parent conference, etc. Seldom is the remedy for bad behavior to be sent away. But for our kids, who were "placed" in the classroom by the IEP team, the most common reaction is to start talking about removing them to a more restrictive placement.

Much can be made of the details and philosophy of behavioral support. This is not the place to write a long and detailed thesis. You need to know these plans are part of the arsenal of advocacy tools that IDEA provides. They need not be made too complicated. Find out what's causing the bad behavior and fix it.

What Is Positive Behavior Support?

Positive behavior support is simply finding and rewarding good behavior instead of punishing bad behavior. Experts often describe it as the opposite of "treating the symptom and not the disease." Trying to punish and modify bad behavior without looking at its cause will only result in a big dose of frustration for everyone.

Why is the behavior happening? Why won't your child stay in his or her assigned seat? Why do they try to leave the classroom? Why do they shout? Why do they engage in injurious behavior? Why do they act like hellions?

Sometimes it is quite easy to see why a child with a disability exhibits bad behavior. When a child throws objects around the classroom it seems pretty clear that the child is attempting to get attention. Punishing children for throwing objects, without learning why they do what they do, puts into motion a spiraling and circuitous series of actions preordained for failure.

Are classmates ignoring the child? A positive behavior support plan creates a strategy to assist the child and his/her classmates to interact better. Is the child eating lunch alone? No one to play with at recess? The best modification for attention getting behavior is to address its cause.

We have all engaged in what educators call "challenging" behavior. And there is a reason for that. Often it works. We do get more attention. Throwing a fit can mean less work, shorter hours, or more personal contact with others. You can easily disrupt another person's schedule by making messes and leaving them for others to attend to.

The goal is to help the child learn better ways to make their needs and feelings known.

Assemble a Team

Be proactive when you learn that your child is behaving in a disruptive or potentially dangerous way. Approach the classroom teacher, express your concern and ask for help and suggestions. Most school districts have staff trained in behavior supports. Find and read resource material, talk to other parents, join an Internet list serve and network with others. Generally there are other parents who have faced the same situation. They can be of great help.

Invite family, friends, professionals, neighbors, educators or anyone else who has contact with your child to offer ideas. Your personal family values play a paramount role here. Don't agree to some kind of behavior modification that offends your own sense of right and wrong. It is important to involve people on the team who are familiar with you and your family.

What Is a Functional Assessment?

A functional assessment is a way of finding out why the behavior occurs. Finding out why is necessary to change the behavior. This assessment follows discussion of precisely what the behavior is. It is important that everyone agrees on the cause or causes. Technical experts usually work for the school or are available to the school. Once everyone has made the best effort to observe the child in good and bad periods of behavior, and you have identified a pattern that sets into motion the bad behavior, you can brainstorm strategies to avoid the cause.

Behavioral Strategies

The Beach Center on Families and Disability at the University of Kansas has done considerable research on behavioral assessment.

They recommend the following strategies to implement your functional assessment.

Teaching New Skills

Challenging behavior frequently happens because people do not know a more appropriate way to get the result they want. A new behavior is needed.

According to the Beach Center, "The new skill may successfully replace the behavior right from the start or it may take longer. When a flare-up does occur, ignore the behavior problem (in cases of physical injury, it may be impossible and unethical to ignore behavior) and introduce known methods that promote good behavior."

"University of Kansas, Beach Center on Families and Disability, Families and Disability Newsletter, Volume 8, Number 3, Winter, 1997."

What Rewards the Individual?

The functional assessment process requires a lot of observation. The observer should have learned what the person views as rewards. When good behavior happens, it should be rewarded. Using rewards reinforces the possibility that good behavior will happen again and again. Rewards encourage the individual to a have a positive identity.

Altering Environments

Organize the child's environment for success. The goal is to create an environment that encourages desirable behavior. Positive behavioral supports are not designed to avoid all places where challenging behavior might occur. Nor are they intended to simply give in to all the individual's requests. Thoughtful change in environment should result in a diminution of bad behavior. If it does not, change it again.

Changing Systems

Take a look at your system of services to see whether it is as responsive and personalized as possible. Do what you can to make it that way. The Beach Center recommends that teachers request time for collaborative planning. A parent can explain positive support practices that work at home. If the system is not changing as fast as you think it should, you may consider literally changing your system for another, e.g., a new school.

The point to remember is that behaviors happen for a reason. Look to find that reason and fix it. The strategies outlined above are basic. Use your own family's knowledge and expertise. Always be proactive. Do not wait until the situation is beyond remedy.

All children exhibit bad behavior. For "normal" kids, it is considered a part of childhood. But for our kids it can, and is, pointed to as yet another reason why they don't belong. If this sounds like a double standard to you, it is. But it is part of our life.

Bad behavior equals a more restrictive placement. Nip it in the bud.

Chapter 5

ADVOCACY AND PROBLEM SOLVING

"Few things are impossible to diligence and skill."

Dr. Samuel Johnson

Preparing and Having a Meeting
Parent Training and Information Centers
Advocacy Groups
A Primer on Note Taking
Records to Keep at Home
Who, When and How Long?
Some Useful Questions to Ask
How Will I Know that I Understand?
Knowing How to Share Your Own Observations
Walk in the Other Person's Shoes
Common Pitfalls and How to Avoid Them
Keep Talking: How to Avoid Due Process
Final Thoughts on Success

IEP and IFSP meetings are your opportunity to build a school year for your child. These meetings are stressful and time consuming and important. Your goal is to be prepared to make the meeting a success.

Circumstances change during a school year, and, if needed, a review of your plan can be done anytime, but good preparation will minimize multiple meetings and reviews. Don't go into a meeting with the idea that you will fix the plan at a later review.

Special education advocacy and problem solving have become complex and often difficult. You can lessen the complexity and emotional strain by focusing attention on the true purpose of a meeting. Don't let what may seem like a complex agenda discourage you. What you are there for is simple: to create a plan that directs what your child will learn and how she/he will learn it.

Think through what you want before the meeting. What do you want your child to learn? If you are well prepared there is a good chance you will get what you want. Your child and your family are unique. That is why it is called "special" education. Your plan is the specially designed curriculum aimed at the needs of one child at a time.

The plan is an INDIVIDUAL plan. It is not a generic plan for all children with similar disabilities. When you are at the table, keep your focus, and the focus of others, on your child and your child's needs. Beware of one-size-fits-all preplanning by school people. Obviously it is easier and cheaper for them to implement the same plan for all kids. That is not what IDEA is about. At your meeting the focus is on your child. "I appreciate how many children you deal with, but, right now, we are only talking about *Bobbie's plan*."

Special education advocacy is about knowing what you want and having the skills to get it. There are solid, practical things you can do ahead of time to help assure success. These things may not all apply in every meeting. Use them as a beginning point for your personal planning.

Preparing and Having a Meeting

Ideas for Parents

Prepare.

Over the years I have learned a great deal about meeting preparation. Some of what I have learned has come from experience and a good deal of it, from talking with other parents, school personnel, and special education students. One thing I do know is that thorough preparation makes all the difference in the world.

These meetings are emotionally difficult. It is not easy listening to strangers talk about all of your child's deficits. Don't be stampeded into making decisions just to get it over with. Learn to believe that you are an equal partner. You have the absolute right to understand everything that is happening. Ask questions until you do understand.

Never miss an opportunity to talk to other parents. They understand how hard these things are. Gather information from them, listen to their stories. Also, away from the formalities of the actual meeting, professionals are often very helpful in proposing ideas and making suggestions.

Make lists of questions, concerns, and things you want your child to learn. Review your records so that you can recall what services you have received when and who has given them. Organize your materials so that you feel you are setting the agenda.

Think about what modifications will help your child learn. Modifications are changes in the general curriculum that are designed to help your child benefit from his/her educational program.

Remember, progress is not measured by the grades non-disabled kids get. If your child is making "meaningful educational progress" on the IEP goals, they are passing.

When Eleanor was very small, her class studied the Oregon Trail and the complexities of pioneer immigration. At the time that aspect of history was way beyond her ability to understand. We instead focused on the shape of the wagon wheels and spokes. Eleanor was able to participate and made some dynamite wagons. She learned a lot and later, at a time more developmentally appropriate for her, she mastered the Oregon Trail.

Bring a Friend

Bring a friend whom you can trust. Don't do these meetings alone. These sessions can feel like "you against the world." They are a time when you may cry, get angry, frightened, and generally feel off track. Having a trusted friend along to keep you on track, hand you the tissues, take notes, and remind you of all the things you planned to say is invaluable.

Your child's future is determined to a large degree by these meetings. It is not a time to hold back. It is a time to call on your informal support network.

A very desperate family once asked me to help them with their first IEP meeting. Their son had just been diagnosed with autism and was entering kindergarten. They believed he would do best in a "regular" kindergarten.

The school was directing them into a self-contained autism classroom. That was not at all what they wanted. Fear of the unknown was choking them. It was making it impossible to focus on learning the rules and influencing the outcome of the meeting.

I suggested they bring their rabbi to the meeting. "But he doesn't know anything about special education," they replied. But bringing their rabbi communicated to the school people the importance of this decision to their family. A member of the clergy came to guide and to comfort them. That only happens at the most important moments of a family's life. It's a big message.

The meeting was a success; their son has been in mainstream classes since and is now doing well in middle school. This was the most important IEP meeting they have had.

There is nothing wrong with having your hand held. You deserve it.

Parent Training and Information Centers

Parent Training and Information Centers are federally-funded programs that help families obtain appropriate education and services for their children with disabilities. There is at least one of these in every state. As their name indicates, these centers provide training and information to parents and professionals, though precisely what the centers offer varies from state to state. Nevertheless, they are a valuable resource for parents who are looking for training on special education advocacy.

Many of these centers employ parents of children with disabilities who have been trained to act as advocates and organizers for families. The value of these centers lies in their knowledge and experience in dealing with state and local issues, the personalities, and the practices.

Parent Training and Information Centers are a good place to start looking for an advocate to help you with your meeting. Some state centers will provide you with a trained parent advocate to accompany and assist you with your meetings. At the very least they will be able to provide you with training opportunities and valuable information

It is very important for you to connect with these programs. To find the one in your state, you can contact the National Technical Assistance Center, known as the PACER Center, in Minneapolis, MN. (952-838-9000 or 952 838-0190 TTY).

Their web address is http://www.taalliance.org/centers

This site will direct you to the center in your state.

Advocacy Groups

Many parents find it helpful to join and participate in advocacy groups. There are a variety of choices. Some of the better-known organizations focus of big picture issues and others are more focused on specific disabilities. System advocacy is important and has resulted in revolutionary change in the lives of people with disabilities.

When Eleanor was an infant we were invited to join a parent support group. We declined. At the time our feeling was simply that we were not ready for it. Our focus was just on getting from one day to another. These are personal decisions. Don't let guilt or family or group pressures make you do something you do not feel right about.

On the other hand the families and advocates you meet through these groups can be a great source of comfort and support. Many advocacy organizations also sponsor social events for kids and families.

There is strength in numbers. Advocacy organizations will want to recruit you. My own experience with them has been extensive and the outcomes mixed. Don't be afraid to try. At their best, these organizations can be of great importance in arenas such a school funding, transportation, etc.

Other parents are the best source of information on which ones they enjoy and why. Organizations such as The Arc of the United States, United Cerebral Palsy, the Down Syndrome Congress, the Down Syndrome Association, etc., maintain web sites about local affiliates and advocacy opportunities. As in all things, use your own judgment.

A Primer on Note Taking

There is a big difference between taking notes and taking *effective* notes. Like other parts of your meeting preparation planning, note taking will make a difference. These meetings are emotionally difficult. Nervously jotting down page after page of words will not be helpful later. Note-taking is a good job for your support person.

Effective notes make it easier for you to follow-up on decisions that are made. They can help you prepare an agenda for a later meeting to deal with unresolved issues, and of course they become a part of the records you maintain for your child. At the meeting itself, you need to focus on the goals and the outcome. Don't try to do that *and* be a note taker.

These meetings are emotionally charged. Don't count on remembering everything without prompting. Your support person can use your meeting preparation notes (it is ideal to have copies for each of you) to prompt you to remember what you want to achieve.

People sometimes bring tape recorders to meetings. Unless you have a very good reason to do that, such as a disability of your own that makes it necessary, I don't recommend doing this. Taping a meeting ups the confrontation ante, sets a tone of conflict that can give the school people the impression that you don't trust them or that you are preparing a transcript for later litigation. This just makes them defensive and less likely to be flexible and cooperative. Of course, if you need a transcript, you must do what you have to do. But the best special education decisions are made early and informally. You should try every road of cooperation, mutual respect, and honesty with professionals before resorting to taping the meetings.

The second issue with tape recorders is a legal one. If you are going to use a recorder, never do it in secret. There are many conflicting state laws regarding the use of electronic recording devices. In some states, it is a felony to tape record someone without their consent.

What to Review Ahead of Time with Your Note-Taker

Begin by listing who attended the meeting, the date and place. Note whether or not everyone is in agreement as to the purpose of the meeting. What are you there for? Is it to plan next year? Is it to review placement? Who called the meeting?

Write details about decisions that are reached regarding each item on the agenda. Before the meeting ends, read the notes back to the team.

Your notes should summarize the decisions made. Ask the team if they are in agreement and, if they are, put that in your notes.

If there are disagreements you should note them also. Try to write your notes in simple language. Avoid loaded language and accusations.

Be sure to have clear notes about issues that did not get resolved. Distinguish between issues that were left unresolved because of disagreement and those that simply were not dealt with because of time. Use your notes as the basis for an agenda for the following meeting.

The purpose of IEP/IFSP meetings is to create an educational plan for your child, but it is not enough simply to *make* a plan; the team has the responsibility for implementing it as well. Your notes should very specifically list the person who is responsible for implementing the decisions made by the team.

Who should you contact if you have questions or need clarification?

How do you reach them?

Be sure to note that the person named has the authority to carry out the decisions.

Insist on a specific date for the implementation of each decision. Make a note of it, of course. Ask whether or not that timetable is reasonable.

Who on the team has the responsibility to make sure the decision is implemented on time?

Who are you to contact if the timeline is missed?

Often the team does not complete the agenda in one meeting. How will you address the unresolved issues? Is there someone not present at your meeting who will be making decisions? If so, who are they and why were they not present? Will school personnel mail a written response or position to you? Who will it be? When? Is there another plan the team can agree on to address unresolved issues?

Don't leave the meeting without answers to these questions and be sure your notes reflect the answers.

Did the team agree on a date, location, time, and participants for another meeting to deal with unresolved issues? Make a note of it.

After meetings, sit with your note-taker and type the notes immediately, while both of your memories are fresh. When you have finished, sign and date them.

Records to Keep at Home

A key responsibility for parents of children with disabilities is to maintain records of your child's educational experience. The school must keep some records, but they will never be as accessible and complete as those you maintain. It is important to have at your fingertips a record to refer to, and you will, in the years to come, appreciate having thorough records; paper trails are the stuff of good advocacy.

If you wish to review your child's school records, you may. In some cases the district may provide them if you ask. If not, make an appointment to inspect them. You can also make copies, although you will probably have to do so at your own expense. Expect a district person to be present when you inspect or copy records.

At a minimum your home records should include all of the following items for each school year.

- The name of your child's teacher or teachers and contact information.
- Name, address, and phone number of the school.
- The principal.
- The psychologist.
- All related services personnel.
- Your child's special education teacher or teachers.
- Your school district superintendent and the Director of Special Education.
- Members of your school board.
- List the chain of command of your school district. You can find this out from their website or their directory. Include telephone numbers, email, and addresses for easy reference.
- Include a short summary of your child's educational rights under IDEA. Contact your state Parent Training and Information Center to ask if they have a list of these that can be mailed to you. A list of rights will serve as handy reminders when you are reviewing your files.
- Keep in chronological order all evaluations, psychological reports, curriculum, decisions or anything else; the district keeps on your child.
- A copy of every IFSP/IEP you have had.
- Report cards and progress reports.
- A copy of all test results and independent evaluations, if any.
- All letters and notes to and from school personnel. If you are not making copies of these things, you should.
- All written communications with outside professionals such as doctors, lawyers, clergy, insurance people, transportation agencies, advocacy groups, etc.
- Dated notes from your parent/teacher conferences as well as your notes from IEP/IFSP meetings and all informal meetings with school personnel.

- Dated notes from conversations with your child's physician or any other professionals with whom you deal.
- Dated notes on all telephone conversations with school personnel or others about your child.
- Always save emails in a special file on your computer, or print copies to keep.
- Be sure to keep a list of medications being given your child at home and at school. Include the kind of medications, time, and dosage information. In addition, keep a record of the prescription numbers as well as changes in dosage and any change in reaction your child might have.

Records provide a written story of what you have done, said, observed and learned. They are the best way to accurately refresh your recollection of an important event from months or years in the past. Records often mean the difference between a good and bad outcome. Sadly, there are far too many situations in which your memory and the memory of others are not the same. Having a record, especially one made on the day of the disputed conversation, will help establish your memory as the correct one.

There are big turnovers from year to year in school personnel. There is little "institutional memory" from year to year. Your complete and well-organized record file will be a service to the whole team.

Who, When and How Long?

Plan to leave the meeting with a clear picture of who is responsible for implementing your plan and precisely when implementation will begin. The meeting must include a district representative with the authority to commit district resources. Make sure to find out right away whom that person is. Get their name and contact information. Do the same with other team members who have responsibility for implementing the decisions that are made.

Give Fair Notice

By looking to your own demeanor, by behaving with courtesy and respect, you can set a tone for cooperation with school personnel. Sadly, it is sometimes impossible to get along with school people. If trust and communication break down, it is even more important for you to remain calm and refrain from doing or saying anything you will come to regret.

If you plan to bring a lawyer to a meeting, let the school know that ahead of time. Lawyers, like tape recorders, communicate a new level of intensity. Generally, a meeting will not take place if you show up with a lawyer, and the district didn't know it. They have lawyers, too, and will probably want theirs present if you have yours.

The goal here is to get a wonderful education for your child. It is not to play "gotcha" with school people. This process is not about adults and how they get along. It is about children and their educational opportunities. Once again, keep your eye on the prize.

Dress for Success

You are attending a business meeting. The way you dress is a non-verbal communication. You need not dress in a way that makes you uncomfortable. But you should think about what to wear. If your clothes are too shabby, it can give the impression that this is not very important to you. That is the opposite of what you want to communicate. Let everyone know, by body language, preparation and dress, that this meeting is very, very important to you.

Talk to Your Child before the Meeting.

Obviously this is less important the younger your child is. But it doesn't hurt to ask them, if possible, what they would like to learn next year in school. As your child gets older they should attend the meetings. Having your child there can really change the tone. Educators are less likely to focus on negatives if the child is there to hear them.

If your child is coming, it is important that you make sure they know what the meeting is about. They should also be warned that a good deal of the meeting would consist of people talking about them.

What does your child want to learn? What do they think help them to learn? What things can be done to make them feel welcome, comfortable, and accepted? This is about your child's life. Include them early and often.

Talk to School People before the Meeting.

The more you can accomplish informally the better. Talk to your child's teacher and the district representative before the meeting. Get an idea of what they are thinking. If you are happy with your child's placement, and school personnel let you know that they will be recommending a change in that placement, you are then on notice for what to expect at the meeting.

Informal contact before the meeting is also an opportunity to begin to mold outcomes. Give them your input at every chance. If you feel strongly about something, you should let them know. Decisions are made at meetings but they can be influenced in other settings. Be an opportunist!

Ask Questions

At stake is your child's education. You have the right and responsibility to understand everything that is happening. You must speak up whenever something is being said that you do not understand, or if there is information you need. If you don't understand ask. Ask until you understand.

Acronyms present a problem to parents. They are a shorthand way for people to talk. For "insiders," they make perfect sense. You probably use them yourself. But if you are an "outsider," they communicate nothing. Ask the other team members not to use acronyms. If they forget and use them anyway, and they probably will, remind them not to. Many districts have a list of common special education acronyms. Ask for it and look at it. Likely it won't be long before you too are using them.

But the bottom line is to never, ever leave a meeting feeling that you do not know precisely what was decided. You have the right to understand. Here is one place to be truly assertive. When in doubt, ask questions.

Some Useful Questions to Ask About Your Child's IEP/IFSP

Understanding is the key to successful advocacy. Asking questions is one key to understanding. Knowing the right questions to ask will empower you to be an equal participant in your meeting.

Here are a series of questions that we have found useful over the years. We developed notes of these years ago and always review them before meetings. You may not need them all. Add questions of your own.

- How will I know if progress is being made?
- What tools and methods will be used to measure progress?*
- Who is going to implement these tools and methods?
- How often will progress be measured?
- How will the school communicate progress to you?**
- How often will the school communicate with you?**
- What is the best way for you to communicate your observations and thoughts to the school people?**
- How often should you communicate with the school?**
- What is the team going to do if little or no progress is being made on goals and short-term objectives?
- Your child will probably be enrolled in regular education classes at least part of the day. How will special education services be coordinated and by whom?
- What can you do to help your child at home?

At a minimum you must plan to leave your meeting with understandable answers to all of these questions.

These questions should be answered on the IEP/IFSP form.

** The answers to these questions *can* be written on the IEP/IFSP

How Will I Know That I Understand?

Being well informed is the single most important advocacy skill you can have.

Take a look at your IEP/IFSP and see how you would answer the following questions.

- Are there clear statements about what my child can do right now?
- This is called Present Level of Performance (PLOP) and is the baseline to measure progress.
- Do the statements of what he/she can do agree with my own observations? If they don't, why don't they? What am I going to do about it?
- Is what my child is supposed to learn by the end of the year clearly stated?
- Are these things important for my child to work on? Are they reasonable?
- Do I understand how progress will be measured? Do I know how well my child is expected to do on each task?
- When this program was developed, were my ideas taken seriously and incorporated into the plan?
- Do I know the specific educational service that will be provided?
- Do I know how much time each day my child will participate in regular education programs?
- Do I know when these programs will begin and how long they will last?
- What things can I do to help my child succeed?

Remember, an IEP/IFSP is not a contract. It is not binding throughout the entire year. It can be changed. But as long as the plan is in effect, the school must provide the services and resources that are written in the plan. Make sure you know what they are.

Knowing How to Share Your Own Observations

Among the worst feelings a parent can have is the one that tells you that your ideas and hopes did not get into the plan. Preparation is the key. I sat down some time ago and thought about what to do to make sure that our family's wishes, dreams, and values made their way into the plan.

It is not enough to just hope it happens. It is not enough to tell them you want it to happen. You must make it happen.

Bring your written answers to the meeting. They will help assure that you are sharing the important things you planned to share.

- Write down your honest assessment of your child's strengths and weaknesses.
- Be prepared to tell the team of any changes in your child's behavior that you have noticed at home.
- Have there been changes in your family or home that might affect your child's learning?
- How does your child learn best? Verbal? Visual? Hands-on? etc.
- Tell the team what your child likes.
- What has worked well for you as positive reinforcement for your child?
- Are there negative reinforcements that should be avoided?
- How does your child interact with peers?
- What is the level of your child's self-help skills?

Take time at the meeting to get these things on the table. You are the world expert on your own child. No one knows more.

What you share with the team can go a very long way toward a successful school year. Don't be afraid to share the most homely stories. Make sure that your plan reflects the needs, personality, and development of your child. Your input is irreplaceable.

Walk in the Other Person's Shoes

Imagine yourself in the position of the school people. Imagine them in yours. Sometimes misunderstandings can be avoided by appreciating the role each person plays and the pressures we all operate under.

There has never been a single human being born on this earth that, at some point in their lives, said to themselves, "I think I will go to college for 6 years, spend a quarter of a million dollars and go into special education so that I can bully and cheat little disabled kids out of their educational rights."

Everyone in special education entered the field for altruistic reasons. Many of them have family members with disabilities. Over time schools can wear anyone to a frazzle. Sometimes it is good for you to gently remind them of why they are there. Help them to do what is right.

In imagining myself as a special education professional, I put together a little checklist of things to think about. Use it yourself to keep on track. Always focus on the outcome.

Checklist for Families

- Do I believe that I am an equal partner with professionals, accepting my share of the responsibility for solving problems and making plans for my child?
- Am I able to see the professional as a person who is working with me on behalf of my child?
- Do I see my goal, while I interact with professionals, as the mutual understanding of problems so that we can work together to solve them?
- Do I maintain a file of important documents and correspondence so that I have a complete history of services provided to my child and family?
- Do I clearly express my own needs and the needs of my family to professionals in an assertive manner?
- Do I clearly state my desire to be an active participant in the decision-making process concerning services for my child? Do I seek mutual agreement on ways to assure my involvement?
- Do I take an assertive role in planning and implementing my child's plan?
- Do I come to appointments having thought through the information I want to give and the questions I want answered?
- Do I accept the fact that a professional often has a large load of families and students to deal with and not just mine?
- Do I treat each professional as an individual and avoid letting past negative experiences or attitudes get in the way of establishing a good working relationship?
- Do I communicate quickly with professionals who are serving the needs of my child when there are family changes or other notable events in my child's life?
- Do I take the opportunity to communicate with other parents? Do we share stories and successes, and help each other to reduce isolation? Do I generously share the expertise I have gained?

- Do I encourage professionals to communicate with one another and to keep me informed as well?

No checklist can be complete. Maybe there is more here than you need. But it is a good advocacy skill to stop and examine your own behavior from time to time.

Just as it helps us as parents to think of ourselves in the role of professional educator, so, too, it is healthy for them to imagine being us. If you are having problems with professionals, why not share your thoughts on their role and ask them to consider yours?

Here is another checklist. This one is aimed at helping professionals appreciate the strain that families can be under.

Check List for Professionals

It's okay for you to ask professionals to consider the items on this list. In fact, if you are feeling frustrated you can share this list with the team. At the least it will demonstrate the lengths you have gone to, to exercise good faith and preparation.

- Can I imagine myself in this parent's place? Have I mentally reversed roles to imagine how I would feel as the parent of this child?
- Do I see this child as a little human, in more than one dimension? Can I look beyond diagnosis, labeling, and disability?
- Do I remember that this child about whom we are talking is someone the parent loves?
- Do I really believe that the parents are equal to me as a professional and, in fact, are experts on their own child?

- Do I constantly value the comments and insights of parents and make use of their reservoir of knowledge about the child's total needs?
- Do I communicate hope to parents when I judge their child's progress?
- Do I listen to parents, communicating with words, eye contact, and posture that I respect and value their insights?
- Do I ask parents questions, listen to their answers, and respond to them?
- Do I work to create an environment in which parents are comfortable enough to speak candidly to me?
- Am I informed about the child prior to a meeting? Do I place equal value on the parent's time and my own?
- Do I treat each parent I come in contact with as an adult who can understand a subject as well as I can?
- Do I speak plainly, avoiding the jargon of medicine, sociology, education, psychology, or social work?
- Do I make a consistent effort to consider the child as part of a family, consulting parents about the important people in the child's life and how their attitudes and reactions can affect the child?
- Do I distinguish between fact and fiction when I discuss a child's problems and potential with parents?

Common Pitfalls and How to Avoid Them

Commonly you will be much stressed before, during, and after meetings. I hate to say that you should expect this, but the likelihood is that it is true. An unhappy reality of many meetings is the necessity for you to sit quietly while professionals talk about all the shortcomings, inadequacies, deficiencies, and deficits they believe your child has. It is not a pleasant time.

Professionals are also stressed. They frequently have large numbers of meetings to attend. They may be feeling unprepared. Your body language and attitude may put them on edge.

The future of your child's education is always on the line. The stakes are high. People sometimes do not behave well. Getting angry and letting your frustrations overflow will mostly not help. (Some honest tears are something else. Let them flow.)

Your best success will come from being calm. There are things you can anticipate and plan for in advance. Talk to your support person about them.

Have a plan to keep the meeting, and yourself, on track. Always remember that the goal is the best possible school experience for your child.

One of the most common things that throw parents off is a feeling that things are just not making sense. Professionals can talk too fast; they can use acronyms and other unfamiliar terms. It can easily feel that the meeting is simply getting away from you.

This is the time for you to remember and believe that you have the right to be there. You have the right to understand everything that is said and done. This isn't about you. It is about your child. Your child frequently cannot act as his or her own advocate. It is up to you. When you feel overwhelmed, take a breath and remember that you have no choice. If you do not handle these meetings in a way that will put your child's interests first, no one else will.

If things aren't making sense to you, stop the meeting. This is important, so I'll repeat it. Stop the meeting. Hold your hand up and say, "Excuse me." Ask people to define the issues, define precisely what it is they are talking about. Make sure the whole team is talking about the same thing. Does the person speaking have the authority to do what they are saying?

Ask if you may have the proposed solution in writing. You should not concern yourself with time efficiency here. This is the time to consider the needs of your child. No other issue is on the table. Know the rules. Challenge "facts" that are offered up with which you do not agree.

We once had a meeting where the district representative kept referring to our daughter as "him." Obviously he was focused on the wrong child. This embarrassed the other members of the team, and we got through it with some mutual eye raising and sly smiles. We did not allow the meeting to break down by accusing him of being unprepared. Basically the other school personnel simply ignored him.

But sometimes you are simply treated rudely, unethically, or disrespectfully. This is one reason to bring a friend. It is simply easier to deal with these things if you are not alone. Seek help from other professionals within the agency. See if they will intervene or, perhaps, assign another person to your team.

Remember that you are not a prisoner. If the team will not allow you to ask questions, understand what is happening, or treats you in a way that makes you feel attacked you can always ask for a break. Sometimes that is all it takes.

Another option is to declare the meeting over and leave. If you do this, be sure to do it politely and explain your reasons. "You have made me feel so angry I can't go on. Another day will be better."

"I am unable to tolerate the attitude toward me and my family. I am sorry. We will just have to reschedule." Terminating a meeting certainly communicates that there is a line over which you will not be pushed. It is reasonable for you to demand respect.

Sometimes parents feel a sense of the "fast shuffle" by school personnel. Sometimes there is just something about a school person that makes it hard for you to work with them.

Always document your numerous attempts to talk things over with the person or persons you are having trouble with. Do not go to supervisors until you have exhausted all reasonable chances of working things out. If you have tried, and can prove you have tried, you will get a more satisfactory hearing from supervisors. Going up the "chain of command" is a last resort.

Bring a written agenda to even the most informal meeting and don't be afraid to bring that all-important friend/helper.

Keep Talking: How to Avoid Due Process

The dream of IDEA is a free and appropriate education for every child. It is a simple concept. It seems that children could often implement it more easily than adults. Sadly, once adults, agencies, budgets, and egos get involved, and they do, a simple dream can become a jangle of conflict and bitterness.

There are procedural and statutory remedies for these conflicts, and they are not fun. Seldom, if ever, are a child's needs served by adult conflict. That said, however, there are exceptions where conflicts are necessary to improve the educational opportunities for our children.

Protecting our right to test educational law in federal court is one of the most important principles of IDEA. The fact is that your children, and you, are almost always better off by letting someone else do that.

Due process hearings are the last step. They are litigation in federal court. Federal court is where these things end up. You have heard the saying, "don't make a federal case of it." There are good reasons for that. Do not threaten the schools with Due Process. Sometimes, unfortunately, this is the only resort. Consult an experienced lawyer before proceeding. This is not a step to be taken lightly.

These hearings are costly, time consuming and emotionally wrenching. Before taking the plunge make sure you are keeping your eye on the prize. And the prize is your child's education. The prize is not "victory" over the school district. The best dispute resolution is the earliest and most informal one.

The best tool you have is attitude. Do not be afraid to laugh – sometimes that is the best response to what you hear. The people who work in the system and the system itself are not the same thing. The system can be ridiculous. But people who work in it are not. Develop relationships with professionals you can trust. Those people can be valuable allies who will tell you what to do to get around some seemingly inviolable district policy. Protect them in your dealings with others.

Try to always separate the person from the system. School personnel are almost always just implementing policy, as they understand it. Evil people don't go into special education. You can perform a powerful deed by saying, once in a while, something like "I know this system can seem downright evil. I don't blame you for its shortcomings. I know you went into this work to help people."

Do not relive the past. Put old disputes behind and move ahead. Be firm in your objectives, but be flexible and creative in brainstorming ways to get there. Try to find areas of agreement and build on them.

167

Body language can help avoid problems. Sit up and listen and don't roll your eyes or made little asides to your support person. This advice may seem too obvious to mention, but people have done it, and, not surprising, it works against them. The way you receive and share information communicates a lot. Unspoken tensions can poison a meeting more than anything else.

Keep your records up to date. Remember that information is power. Have yours ready to use.

Professionals love test scores and assessments. Our children typically do not do well on tests. If you are unprepared, with your own evidence, you can be defeated by tests scores that "prove" your child cannot do the things you know he or she can do. Counter this by keeping representative samples of your child's schoolwork. These samples can demonstrate that your child is benefiting from his or her educational placement.

The real test is whether or not your child is making meaningful educational progress on his or her goals. Your child is not required to match up with their non-disabled peers.

Join an organization. There is power in numbers. There are lots of advocacy organizations. Find one in your community that has a newsletter and opportunities for training for parents.

Believe in yourself before all else. This isn't easy. But you can do it. Our family did and millions of others as well. So can you. Come to believe that you are an equal participant in decision-making. Ask what is important to yourself and your family. Prepare what you want in writing.

The ultimate goal of IDEA is to reduce dependency on others. Know what your child is capable of. Know how your child learns best. Know what changes are necessary in your educational plan to make learning happen. Use these things as your foundation as an effective and respected advocate. And again, remember; keep your eye on the prize.

There is no substitute for good preparation.

Final Thoughts on Success

Remember that schools are established as a service to your community. Special education cannot be healthier than the school system as a whole. Your strong involvement in the school will go a long way toward assuring quality services for all children. Participate in PTA, advisory groups, and fund raisers. Be a part of the school community.

You are the primary and most important teacher, observer, record keeper, supervisor, and decision maker for your child. If you feel resistance from the school in they're including you as an equal, try not to react with anger. Your child is best served when you, the teacher and other personnel have developed a positive working relationship that allows for snags and disagreements to be dealt with in a calm and rational way.

Try to find someone who can help you coordinate your various diagnosis and services. Pick the person with whom you have the best relationship. Pick someone who understands your role as the primary person in your child's life. A friend, teacher, case manager or advocate can do this for you.

You can't start too early. As soon as you know you have a child with a disability, start keeping a notebook. Keep the names and addresses of people you work with. Make notes of phone calls. Include the date, purpose, and results of visits and conversations. Make important requests by letter and keep a copy. Document every step of your effort to get your child appropriate services. You will never be able to hold anyone accountable if you cannot remember their name, the date you talked or met, and the purpose of the call or meeting.

Be a good educational citizen. Get to know other parents in the school. Believe in yourself and your child.

You are the foremost expert in the world on your child. Learn to act like it. This is not easy and it is not a path that most of us choose. But it is the path you are on. You can master this. Don't be afraid to laugh or cry. They are equally helpful. But never give up.

You cannot undo some things. But you can lay the foundation for the happiest and most independent life possible for your child. And that makes it all worthwhile.

Chapter 6

INCLUSION

"Inclusion is a battle cry,
a parent's cry,
a child's cry to be
welcomed,
embraced,
cherished,
prized,
loved as a gift,
as a wonder
a treasure."

Marsha Forest
1942 – 2000

Philosophy
Using IDEA as a Strategy for Inclusion
Barriers to Overcome
Building Inclusion into Your IEP
Building Inclusion During the Meeting
Building Inclusion After the Meeting
Building Inclusion into Your goals
Examples of well written goals
Words to use
Implementing Inclusion: How to Evaluate Your IEP
Using Supplemental Aids and Services
Promoting Inclusion by Using the law
Curriculum Modification
Additional Strategies That Make Inclusion Work
The Full Inclusion Battle Song

Philosophy

The word "inclusion" does not appear anywhere in IDEA. It is not a legal term. Inclusion is a dream. In this dream, all people matter and all people have a contribution to make. A contribution to their family, their school and their world. Inclusion is acceptance that not all of us look, talk, walk, or think exactly alike. The dream of inclusion means that our common humanity makes differences a source of pride and strength and not something to shamefully hide under a basket.

Inclusion of children with disabilities is a composite of dreams and hopes that come from a rich variety of sources. Inclusion is the opposite of exclusion.

Prior to the Education of the Handicapped Act in 1954, there was no acceptance of the notion that public schools had any obligation to educate kids with disabilities. Of course, in those days, most children with disabilities were separated from their families at birth and sent to live out their years in state run institutions.

John is a friend of mine. I have known him over half my life and we have shared some very important times together. He is a warm, sweet, and very thoughtful man. When Eleanor was young our family went to visit him in Southern Oregon. I was surprised at his behavior. He was uncomfortable, distant, and nervous in her presence.

It turned out that he had a secret. Before he was born his parents had a daughter with Down syndrome. She was sent off to live in an institution in Michigan. Experts had convinced them that it would be best for all concerned. All John had ever heard about his sister was that she had been removed from all contact with her family because it was "for the best."

When he saw little Eleanor, all full of stories, delights and joy, he realized, for the first time, that his sister was a real person with potential and a need for family and love. By then she was dead.

This is one of millions of stories of broken families and misplaced "advice" from experts. To an extent, inclusion is simply a reaction to the exclusion of the past.

A serious attempt to close institutions began in the 1970s. Prior to that time hundreds of thousands of children with disabilities were separated and isolated in them. Today many states have closed their institutions and many others have stopped accepting children. Today there are fewer than 2,000 children in institutions in the USA.

The closure of institutions led to a dramatic increase in the number of children with disabilities who live at home with their families. This increase in kids in the community happened at the same time that IDEA, and its mandate that all children have the right to a free and appropriate public education, caused parents and educators to attempt to educate kids with disabilities along with other "regular" neighborhood children.

This increasing number of children with disabilities living, for the first time in large numbers, in close contact with the communities in which they were born is one of numerous progenitors of the educational and personal philosophy we call inclusion.

Another influence is educational reform. IDEA is just one of many educational reforms that have and are changing the way children are being educated. Demographics have led to the creation of curriculum for English as a Second Language. That too is controversial. Many people argue that children learn best in the language spoken in their home. Others worry that the "melting-pot" role that public schools have historically played with our immigrant population is put at risk. Curriculum has changed. All change brings controversy. Historical evidence aside, there are many people who take offense to the idea that maybe Columbus did not "discover" America in 1492 and that, in fact, there were thriving human civilizations when he arrived. Change and controversy are, seemingly, twins. And if there is one constant in the world, it is change.

New ways of thinking about education in general is another contributor to our modern notion of inclusion of all children, regardless of disability.

Something that may surprise many readers is the fact that it is now easier than ever to raise a child with a disability. Not too long ago a child with a disability was seen as a problem that rested exclusively with his/her family. In the past few decades both the federal and state government have recognized the unique strains on families that having a member with a disability can cause. Today most states have some form of family support program. Supplemental Security Income and Medicaid play a large role in the financial lives of many people and families. Accessible public buildings and transportation have made it easier than ever for many formerly isolated individuals to be a part of a community. Inadequate and rule bound as these programs may be, they are a whole lot better than nothing.

So governmental action and political reform must also be recognized as a source for the "revolution of rising expectations" that many call inclusion.

There has also been a corresponding change in the measurement and appreciation of human potential. We have learned, that with proper supports, people with the most severe disabilities are able to make contributions thought impossible a generation ago. From his wheelchair, Justin Dart, Jr. moved a nation to pass the Americans with Disabilities Act. Using a sophisticated combination of computers, communication boards, and eye activated assistive technology; Steven Hawking has explained cosmology to the world. Today's parents look at their child with a disability and imagine them living independently and being real, contributing members of our society.

175

An increase in understanding of the mystery of human development has its part in forming the inclusion movement that so many families have embraced.

The 1960s saw enormous changes in the lives of Afro-Americans. The whole notion of civil rights came to the forefront of American life in an unprecedented way. The Civil Rights Movement led the way for many other groups to assert themselves. The movement for gender equity came from groups of women seeing parallels in their lives with those of segregated and marginalized communities like those that emerged from the Civil Rights Movement. Gays and lesbians, senior citizens, racial minorities of all kinds have come to expect a whole piece of the American dream. People with disabilities are no exception.

IDEIA is a civil rights act in name as well as deed.

The belief in inclusion as a civil right is another factor in the educational philosophy that we call inclusion.

These factors alone, and in combination, have given a generation of parents some dreams and plans for their child with a disability that were unheard of a generation ago. And, since IDEIA only requires schools to provide an educational program designed to make "progress" on educational goals, this relatively low standard collides with family dreams in ways that are often dramatic.

Using IDEA as a Strategy for Inclusion

Although the word inclusion does not appear anywhere in IDEIA, that law does provide you with the tools necessary to make inclusion of your child possible.

The first step is for you to decide if this is what you want. At first glance it may seem hard for you to imagine your child being included in a class with non-disabled kids. Experience shows that they can be. By using the tools of IDEIA you can create an IEP that will result in placement in a regular classroom with regular kids. All it takes is some imagination, perseverance, and skill. And a strong belief in yourself, your family values and a rich future for your child.

To successfully achieve your goal of an inclusive education you need to apply some of the things that were discussed in Chapter 3. What tools can IDEIA give you?

IDEIA requires schools to provide special education and related services appropriate to the unique needs of each student with a disability. The IEP must be designed to enable the child to benefit from his/her education.

What does IDEIA mean by "educational benefit"? It means that the child with the disability is making meaningful progress on his or her IEP goals. It does not mean that your child must "pass" regular tests or compete head on with non-disabled peers. Because of curriculum modification (discussed below), your child's progress is not measured by a normal grading system. You have succeeded in your placement as long as your child is "benefiting."

Once an IEP is developed that is tailored to meet your child's unique needs, the school is under a legal obligation to provide the instruction in the "least restrictive environment." The current version of IDEIA requires the IEP team to list the blocks of time the student will not spend in the general curriculum. In legal terms the "burden of proof" is now on the school to justify self-contained classrooms.

These "least restrictive environment" rules are there to help you form your argument as to why an inclusion placement is appropriate. What does "least restrictive environment" mean?

First, placement must not be based on a category of disability, administrative convenience, availability of services, curriculum content or the organization of a service delivery system. IDEA prohibits the creation of "one size fits all" placements. Schools cannot simply shuffle all children with autism into their "autism classroom" any more than they can create a "Down syndrome" room.

It cannot be repeated too often that the IEP must be designed for one child at a time!

IDEIA requires schools to provide a continuum of placements to meet the needs of students with disabilities to whatever extent necessary to implement an IEP. Specifically, these services must be available to all students with disabilities, even those with the most severe disabilities.

Your child cannot be removed from the regular education environment unless the school can demonstrate that, even with the use of supplementary aids and services, your child cannot benefit. Supplementary aids and services may include the use of a resource room, instructional assistants (commonly called Aids) peer tutoring, supported education consultants, etc. And remember, benefit only means progress on the IEP. It does not require that goals be met.

Before removing your child to a more restrictive placement, the school must consider potential harmful effects on your child or on the quality of the services to be delivered. Think about potential harm as a larger question than simple academics. The goal of IDEA is to make your child as independent and self-supporting as possible when they are adults. The world is full of people without obvious disabilities. Learning to function in that world is essential. While it may be tempting to give up if there are problems today, it is more important to remember the long-term goal. Any child can succeed in an inclusion placement if there are appropriate supports and modifications.

While it is true that regular class placement is not appropriate if the student with disabilities is so disruptive that the education of other students is significantly impaired, it is also true that there are rules about discipline that are specific to children with disabilities. (See Chapter 7 for a discussion of "Discipline and Removal"). A disruptive child cannot be removed until positive behavioral support plans have been tried and failed. And it is a rare case where success cannot be achieved if all parties work together to make it happen.

Barriers to Overcome

The first barrier that will be thrown up at you is a continuing reluctance of many school districts to place children with mental retardation in regular classrooms where academic subjects are taught. Attack this objection by reminding them that the issue is not whether your child can compete academically but whether they are making progress on the IEP goals. The supports your child is entitled to include the use of supportive aids and services, including an educational assistant. (Commonly referred to as the "aid.") Providing special education in a regular classroom is part of the continuum of educational placements the law requires of schools. As surely as schools must develop curriculum that reflects cultural diversity, so too must they develop curriculums that reflect cognitive diversity.

Another common barrier is the school's reluctance to provide an educational assistant for your child. Remember that placements cannot be made on administrative convenience! The school will never characterize their wishes this way. More commonly they will tell you that educational assistants foster an over dependence on adults. But that is an issue for staff training. It does not have to be that way. Educational assistants can also be assigned to a classroom and not just to one student. Basic staff training of educational assistants can prepare them for interventions with your child in appropriate and nonintrusive ways.

Don't allow this objection to go unchallenged. Ask for data that supports the conclusion that your child has developed an unhealthy dependency on their educational assistant. What has the school done to curb that over dependence?

Some students will necessarily be dependent on peers and adults. How would this differ in a self-contained classroom? In which placement are peers more likely to provide natural supports to your child? The balancing test the IEP team must use is a determination of the risk of over reliance with the potential benefit of more inclusion. This is what advocacy is about.

What is the appropriate peer group for your child? It has always struck me as odd that schools place children with severe emotional problems in a classroom full of other children with severe emotional problems. Does that constitute an appropriate peer group? This argument can be summarized as "they belong with their own kind." That was the argument for institutions. It is a violation of IDEA to assume that only individuals with severe disabilities comprise a socially appropriate peer group for other individuals with severe disabilities.

Schools will try to convince you that the programs offered in "specialized" placements are "better." Naturally we all want the best. But this is a false argument not supported by the law. This would be placement based on administrative convenience. School districts cannot impose restrictive placements on students simply because of the prospect of "better" programming in the more restrictive placement. The correct question is: What is the least restrictive placement that will confer some – not necessarily the best – educational benefit, without causing harm to fellow students.

Lack of resources is another oft-cited barrier to an inclusive placement. It is worth noting that the law we are dealing with is not the "Disability Education Act." It is the "Individuals with Disabilities Education Act." The educational needs of one student at a time are the main driver of IDEA. School budgets are important. There are opportunities in the political arena for you to work for adequate educational funding. Sacrificing your child's education is not required. Those are two very separate issues.

Building Inclusion into Your IEP

The IEP drives your services! The last thing an IEP team does is to make a placement decision. A clever advocate creates an IEP with goals and services that can only be implemented in an inclusive placement. There are ways to make sure this happens.

The first thing is for you to have clear goals. If you want an inclusive education for your child, make it your priority to support every opportunity to develop relationships with children who do not have disabilities. These are referred to as "natural supports" and are an essential part of everyone's life.

It is hard for parents to imagine just what supports are. You may be afraid to ask for them. Everyone has them. Everyone has supplemental aids. Imagine a meeting in a typical conference setting. One person attends in a wheelchair. One way to characterize that meeting is to say that the person with the wheelchair brought his or her own chair. All others had to be "accommodated." The room where the meeting took place was lighted with a complicated and expensive system of electrical hookups and wires that run all the way back to a dam or power source. That accommodation is not necessary for a blind person.

Electric lights are simply an accommodation for sighted people. Your child's need for accommodation is not so unique, complicated, or expensive.

Before the meeting, get to know the key people. Key people include parents who share your vision of inclusive education. If possible get to know and talk to other members of the IEP team and let them know your wishes.

Some suggested ways to prepare and organize your input for an inclusive placement:

- Make a list of your child's strengths and weaknesses. Include input from family members, friends, and others who know your child.
- List your child's needs and things you would like your child to do better. Think about the kinds of environments and/or supports that your child needs to learn new skills.
- Think of goals that reflect your priorities and think of ways that each could be taught in a regular classroom environment. ADVOCACY TIP: When writing goals include phrases such as "with typical peers used for support," "with one prompt from a typical child," "in the presence of children without disabilities." Obviously, once adopted these goals can only be implemented in an inclusive placement.
- In determining how appropriate a goal may be, choose those that may interest a typical student the age of your child.
- Is the goal age-appropriate? Going to see Santa will appeal to non-disabled peers who are 6. When they are sixteen that is not an appropriate goal.
- What methods are necessary to teach my child appropriate skills?
- How will my child use new skills to increase opportunities to participate in the community?
- Document times where inclusion has worked successfully for your child. Video or photograph family vacations, church activity, etc.

- Request that evaluations be done by people with expertise in supported education. Remember that evaluation results often include placement recommendations. Ask the evaluator to include a description of accommodations and supports that will enable your child to participate successfully with typical peers. Remember that if you disagree with the results, you have the right to ask for an independent evaluation.

Building Inclusion During the Meeting

Share your vision and expectations clearly with the team.

Keep the focus on your child's strengths.

Use words carefully but forcefully. Be assertive, clear, and concise. State the things that *you* want; "building relationships is a priority...needs experience learning in a group...develop friendships with children in our neighborhood...participate in all fourth grade activities...needs behavior models from typical kids,"

Evaluate carefully what is being written. The amount of time not spent in the regular classroom must be listed.

Ask yourself questions: How can this skill be taught in a regular classroom? Consider privacy and dignity – some skills may need to be taught in a different environment.

Bring an advocate. Another parent who shares your vision of inclusion is an ideal advocate. But anyone in your life that you trust is also ideal. Outline roles and strategy ahead of time. Who will take notes? Who has the tissues? Who will suggest a break?

Consider designating a member of the team as a facilitator to make sure things happen day-to-day and that the IEP really gets implemented.

If appropriate, consider some kind of collaborative planning process. Consider these questions:

- What is my child's history?
- What are my dreams for my child?
- What are my nightmares about my child?
- Who is my child?
- What are my child's strengths, gifts, and abilities?
- What are my child's individual needs?
- What would my child's ideal day at school look like?
- What must we do to make that day a reality?

Work as a team member and support the team.

Building Inclusion After the Meeting

Stay involved—every day!

Keep in touch with school personnel. Perhaps a communication notebook could be sent home daily or weekly. Telephone. Schedule informal conferences, meeting, and updates.

Give staff positive feedback throughout the year. School personnel are human, too!

Have a continuous informal reevaluation process underway. Is this working? Are the supports we agreed to really being provided? Are we making friends? Is the IEP really a learning guide? Is my child happy? Do we need to change the IEP?

If necessary ask for an IEP review. The IEP is subject to change at any time.

Most important: Believe in yourself and your family's dream for your child!

Building Inclusion into Your Goals!

Special education advocacy is far more art science. Nowhere is this truer than in writing the goals for the IEP. Here is where inclusion gets written into the document in a way that will require an inclusion placement in order to implement the goals. This is fundamental. Don't wait for the end of the meeting when the placement decision is made. You will not receive an inclusive placement if your goals can be met in a more restrictive setting.

Former Oregon Advocacy Center staff attorney Suzy Harris taught me the most important rule about writing goals: ***Never write a goal that a dead person can meet!***

"Adria will sit quietly in her chair" is not an educational goal. It is a postmortem.

185

Goals must be written in an active voice and state specifically what your child is going to learn. Think about the difference between these written goals.

"Taylor will take piano lessons."
Or
"Taylor will learn to play the piano."

"Grendahl will attend 20 specialized reading classes."
Or
"Grendahl will increase his/her reading skill to a 2nd grade level by attending 20 specialized reading classes."

The first example tells us little about a measurable outcome. In the second, the students, Taylor and Grendahl, are actually setting a goal to be able to perform a very specific and measurable skill. The second goal is written positively.

One important tactic for you to learn and employ is to get the team to buy into IEP goals, one at a time, so that once the document is adopted, it will lead to an inclusion placement. If you include enough references to social situations, support from non-disabled peers, and the need for normalcy, you will have created in IEP that cannot be implemented anywhere other than in an inclusion placement.

Some Specific Examples of Well-Written IEP Goals

"Rachel will learn to walk from her home to school with the support of non-disabled peers by Christmas break."

"Annie will learn three exercises in the company of and supported by non-disabled peers in the afternoon dance class."

"Ephriam will learn number recognition to 10 using adapted materials while participating in regular third grade math."

"Meredith will learn, with support from non-disabled peers, to tolerate distractions during the eighth grade health class and in the lunchroom."

"Daniel will interact and participate actively with typical children in tenth grade social studies and science."

Some Words to use for Specific Skills

Motor goals
Play on the soccer team.
Drive a car.
Use scissors.
Perform in a recital.
Learn to swim.

Social/Emotional goals
Display good manners.
Sleep with the lights on.
Play with peers.
Participate in board games.

Vocational Goals
Be on time.
Do household chores.
Learn to type.
Follow instructions.

Goals must be clear and positive. Think about what you are saying? Does it specify the skill to be learned? Is it really what you want?

Is "Skye will learn to cross the street safely 90 percent of the time," really what you intended to write?

Implementing Inclusion: How to Evaluate Your IEP

Review your IEP and ask yourself whether or not the goals and objectives have clearly measurable outcomes. Do you understand the criteria? Fifty percent of what? Eighty percent of what? What is expected of the student in order to master the goal? How, exactly, does one measure a goal such as increased independence? What is the next step?

Keep track of progress. How often will your child be tested and what methods will be used? You have the right to a written progress report at least as often as regular education children get report cards. These progress reports can be provided much more often if the IEP calls for them. If you have an educational assistant, ask them (or have the IEP require them) to give you daily written updates on behavior, progress on goals, and other specific homework assignments. Using assistive technology goals, you can ask for and receive a laptop computer that comes home with your student. Daily notes can be recorded on a "desktop" file and you can respond in writing. That keeps you current without the need for a personal contact or phone call everyday.

The amount of time spent on a service should be specific. For direct services check your IEP to see whether or not you have included the minutes per session and the number of sessions per week. The amount of time spent, in specialized reading, for example, must reflect your child's needs. It cannot simply be a categorical amount that applies to all special education students in your school.

The amount of service is a decision for the IEP team to make. It is not a decision of the therapist. Of course, the therapist may make recommendations. The amount of service does not imply "pull-out," one-on-one, or small group learning. Consider this your goal. Bringing a friend or non-disabled peer, or both, to a pullout session increases opportunities for socialization, natural supports, and communication goals. Use your imagination to get what you want.

Do not assume that consultation time mentioned in the IEP will happen. Make sure the consultation time is very specific. Example: "Speech therapist will consult for thirty minutes per month with adapted PE specialist on use of tangible communications system for use during Adapted PE class."

Specialists are busy and often do not have time to talk to each other. Do not just assume that they do. Write their consultation requirements into the IEP or as part of a detailed implementation plan.

Using "Supplemental Aids and Services" as Part of an Inclusion Strategy

"Supplemental aids and services" are those necessary to ensure the student's participation in his/her educational program. These are decided upon by the IEP team and must be done at the IEP meeting right after the goals and objectives have been adopted. These are very important because they spell out specifically just what aids and services the school is obligated to provide in order to assure the successful implementation of your IEP. Parents wonder just what they may ask for and what is available. The list is endless but here are examples of supplemental aids and services that may be used by the IEP team to assure participation in your child's educational program.

A positive behavioral support plan or behavior management plans.

An "individual physical management plan" is a supplemental aid or service. Examples are feeding protocols, toileting issues, proper positioning, etc.

Emergency protocols. Who is your physician? What is the name of your health insurance policy and the phone number for the hospital? Who should be notified first and second and third in the event of an emergency? How can they best be reached?

Individual health plan of support. If there are respiratory or other health needs during the day, who will provide them and how? What about prescription medications?

What adaptive equipment is necessary? Who will provide it? Does it need to be designed for a specific need? Can someone make quick repairs on a wheelchair?

Is there an accessible toilet or drinking fountain in close proximity to classroom and/or playground? Can your child's aid have a key to conveniently located adult bathrooms for your child's needs?

Is the playground equipment accessible? If not what is the plan to make it so? An IEP goal calling for recreation with non-disabled peers cannot be met if the playground equipment excludes your child.

Is there a concrete, tangible, communication system in place so that you know what is happening daily, weekly? How does it work? Who is responsible?

If there is an educational assistant, what training has she or he had? Does your child require someone who has had training in seizure management? What about physical management? Does the EA know how to operate a communications system? If not, who will provide that training and when? Is there a concern about first aid skills, structured teaching, autism skills, etc? What is the backup system in the event the EA is absent?

Is there a time-out or break room near the classroom? How will it be used? Who will decide? Are you in agreement with this tactic?

If there are to be workbaskets, visual calendars, etc employed as visual organizational systems, what are they and who will create them? Is that person trained and qualified?

If your child is deaf or hard of hearing what kind of communication system will be used? Who in the classroom is a qualified sign language interpreter?

Who will do ongoing curriculum modification and provide hands-on activities?

What about the development of parallel curriculum using age-appropriate materials?

Will supports from non-disabled peers be provided through some sort of buddy system or circle of friends? If so, who organizes that? How will it work? Will it be in place all day or just during vulnerable times, such as before and after school, recess, lunch, etc.?

Will there be regular team meetings to look at implementation issues, teaching strategies, consistency, problems, and problem solving?

The important thing is specificity. The listing of supplemental aids and services should not leave things to convenience or interpretation. Make sure they will happen, and know how, when, and by whom.

If you think your child needs a one-on-one educational assistant, a good way to get it is by writing a job description for just what that person will do all day. Educational assistants can be of great help in implementing your goals and promoting the success of your child. By writing up a job description you will generate ideas that can go into the "accommodations, modifications" section of your IEP.

Promoting Inclusion by Using the Law

Inclusion does not appear anywhere in IDEA. What IDEA does require is placement in the least restrictive environment. What test does an IEP team have to employ to determine compliance with the least restrictive environment requirement?

You don't have to be a lawyer to do this work. This is not a law book. However, it may be helpful to you if we review a federal case on least restrictive environment and see how the facts were applied to come up with a balancing test that, in the opinion of the Court, satisfied the legal requirement. This case may or may not be the law in your federal circuit. But it does provide a background analysis that you can urge on your IEP team if appropriate.

The case is commonly referred to as the *Holland* case. (Sacramento City Unified School District Board of Education v. Rachel H. Holland, 18 IDELR 761, 9th Circuit Court of Appeals, [1994]).

At the time of the litigation, Rachel Holland was an eleven-year-old student with mental retardation. At her IEP meeting, her family asked that she be placed in a regular education classroom and the district refused. The district's offer was to place Rachel in regular education classes for non-academic subjects, such as art, music, lunch, and recess. The academic goals on her IEP were to be implemented in a separate special education classroom. Following the procedural guarantees of IDEA, Rachel's parents requested a Due Process Hearing. After hearing the case, the Hearing Officer concluded that the school's proposal was inadequate to satisfy the IDEA requirement of "least restrictive environment." The Hearing Officer ordered the school district to place Rachel in a regular classroom with appropriate support services and supplemental aids, which, in this case, included a special education consultant and a part-time educational assistant. The school district appealed to the US District Court that agreed with the Hearing Officer.

The school district appealed the District Court decision to the US Court of Appeals for the 9th Circuit. (US Courts of Appeal are just one level below the US Supreme Court). The Court of Appeals agreed with the District Court and, in doing so, said that although they were unable to state the appropriate placement for Rachel they would require future IEP meetings to include the following balancing test.

- The child's educational benefits of placement full-time in a regular class.
- The child's non-academic benefit of regular classroom placement.
- The effect the child has on the teacher and children in the regular class, and
- The cost of a general education placement.

Since the Court described this as a balancing test, it is exactly what an IEP team is required to do. They balance these competing issues and assign whatever weight to each of them that they wish.

What is helpful to you with this argument is that the Court required that under IDEA public schools have the obligation to at least attempt a regular classroom placement with supplementary aids and services before trying a segregated placement!

Don't try to pretend you are a lawyer. But be aware that the least "restrictive" environment requirement has some legal teeth behind it. If you succeed in convincing the team that they must at least try an inclusion placement then your effort at supporting its success becomes ever more important. Don't concede that, if the first attempt is a failure, you are preordained to a life in self-contained classrooms. The requirement includes the provision for all sorts of supplemental aids and services that must be provided, tinkered with and implemented before concluding that the placement was inappropriate.

Curriculum Modification

IDEA requires a placement in the least restrictive environment. More and more it is to be expected that students in special education will be educated with their peers in regular curriculum settings. Since there are diverse learning styles, speeds, and capabilities curriculum can no longer be presented in a "one size fits all" model. American classrooms will reflect these diverse learning styles to a greater degree than ever. Adapting curriculum to fit the learning styles and capabilities of diverse learners is called curriculum modification. Modifying curriculum is a basic educational skill.

It is important to remember that there are times when modifications and changes are not required. Students in the same environment and using the same materials should at least be given an opportunity to reach the same-targeted goals. But as academic complexity increases, the need for a modified curriculum will grow.

There are two main ways to modify curriculum and they can occur separately or together.

The first is modified materials. This means that the materials and equipment used to achieve learning outcomes differ. Examples include the use of various output devices to do book reports, computers, calculators and typewriters. The use of Braille machines to do written work is a curriculum modification. Using a tape recorder, or other recording device, in order to take notes is another.

A second type of curriculum modification is "modified learning outcomes." In this model all students work in the same subject area, but some of the students are working at a significantly different level or on different skills. (Remember that your child only has to receive educational benefit from the placement. She or he don't have to earn traditional passing grades.) Examples include doing ten math problems instead of twenty-five, having a spelling list of fifteen words instead of twenty, writing a paragraph and not a page, single words instead of whole sentences. Other possibilities include listening to a book on tape while others are doing silent reading, doing simple addition while others multiply, or identifying letter names while others work on letter sounds.

How does your child learn? What modifications does he/she need in order to be in a regular classroom, studying the same subject but with a different level of learning? This is where believing in yourself and your child will help a lot.

Another curriculum modification can be where the subject being studied (the curricular domain) is different. Students either work in groups or as individuals. Some can be working on one subject and the other group or groups on a different subject. Imagine that all students in the class are at their desk doing worksheets. Some are answering questions from a reading lesson and a few are doing math computations. Cooperative learning groups in which different students are doing different tasks is an example of this type of modification.

Educational objectives may require separate environments for part of the day. The majority of students may be in the general classroom working on geography while one is being tutored in the library, one is in a computer lab and one is in the community learning how to ride a bus.

When thinking of appropriate modifications for your child consider some of these ideas. No one style is always right.

Alter instructional styles used by the teacher. Consider such things as pairing, small groups, large groups, and cooperative learning.

195

(These interactions with non-disabled peers are not only examples of curriculum modification but also make wonderful inclusion goals for your IEP.)

Support structures in the classroom may be changed. Consider the use of peer tutoring, educational assistants, cross age tutoring and teacher's assistants.

Curriculum modification can include changing the classroom environment. Keeping your child seated somewhere visible can be a big aid in bringing him or her into a sense of membership in the class. Obviously physical modifications must be made to assure accessibility. Special lighting may be required. The list is endless.

Additional Strategies That Make Inclusion Work

The first and best strategy is to think about what the system would do with any other child and try that first.

Teachers must model inclusion by calling on and demonstrating that they value the diverse learners in their classrooms. They must take care to include and interact with students with disabilities in regular routines and activities just as they do with everyone else. Teachers can demonstrate to the class that everyone belongs and has value by calling on students with disabilities, talking to them, working with them and assigning them to groups, tables, class jobs, etc.

Consider the use of a buddy system or circle of friends. This can be the whole class or a smaller number of students who are close to the person with the disability. The group can meet on a regular basis to brainstorm, problem solve, build friendships, and plan school and non-school activity. These often become weekly class meetings where the needs of all students are addressed and all students are supported and valued.

Encourage cooperative learning techniques that promote cooperation and the participation of all students of varying abilities.

Curriculum adaptations are ideas that allow all students to actively participate at their own level and meet their own goals in the everyday curriculum. Adaptation is about seeing ways for all students to have a role and take part in the instruction that they need.

A Supported Education Consultant is one who teams with the regular education teacher to provide on-going support and technical expertise on ways to include all students in regular education. Such a person can provide consultation, staff-training, in-service training, and offer expertise on such things as positive behavioral support plans.

An Educational Assistant can also provide additional support. The assistant's role is to act as an aid to the teacher, on behalf of all students; by showing peers ways to interact and include the student with a disability and assist in the management of special needs as necessary. The more the assistant is viewed as a facilitator and classroom assistant, the more the student with the disability will be viewed as just another member of the class.

The IEP team must work with the general education teacher to solve problems, and brainstorm ideas in order to work together for the benefit of all kids.

The Full Inclusion Battle Song

I began this chapter by noting that inclusion is a philosophy rather than a legal requirement and noted that reasons, often cited, for full inclusion are closely linked to those of the Civil Rights Movement. No social movement can be complete without some music of its own.

Mara Sapon-Shevin and Mayer Shevin are disability rights and human rights activists who are also wonderful musicians and composers. Here, for your inspiration and amusement is one of their compositions in support of inclusive education. It is used with permission.

THE FULL INCLUSION BATTLE SONG

Sung to the tune of "Union Maid"
© Mara Sapon-Shevin, Mayer Shevin
Used with permission

There once was a boy named Mike, an easy kid to like,
He went to school just down the block
Where the kids didn't care how he walked or talked.
But then the District said, "This kid needs special ed,"
You could hear the scream for miles around
When the mom reared back and said.

Oh, you can't scare us we're fighting for inclusion,
We're winning and you're loosing, it's our future that we're choosing.
Oh, you can't scare us we're fighting for inclusion,
We're fighting for inclusion, and we all know why!

The screening team got mad, at the weird ideas mom had,
"We don't see why these parents mind
This kid belongs with his own kind.
The special school is great, he'll learn to bowl and skate."
But the more they tried to change mom's mind
The more she got irate.

CHORUS

The head of special Ed, pulled out his file and said,
"Just look at these IQ statistics, these parents must be realistic.
Our job is to protect this child from gross neglect"
But the parents held their ground and said,
"We mean no disrespect, but…"

CHORUS

But back at Michael's school the kids could not be fooled,
They said "we want our classmate back"
They gave the teacher's lots of flack.
"We know that Mike is slow, but he shouldn't have to go."
The teachers said, "But you're just kids"
The kids all said, "We know!" but…

CHORUS

When the hearing came around, the family
Stood their ground.
They brought the folks from PEAK
And fourteen kids from down the street.
The judge said, "I can see, and I'm sure you'll all agree
I have no doubt where Mike belongs"
Then he joined in with this song.

CHORUS.

My friend Dan Wilkins from Ohio said it best. "Mainstreaming," he said, "is visiting. Inclusion is belonging."

Sing, be happy and proud, have a sense of humor, believe in your family, its values, hopes, and dreams. Remember, you can do this!

Chapter 7

CONFLICT RESOLUTION AND DISCIPLINE

"When in doubt, make a fool of yourself.
There is a microscopically thin
line between being brilliantly creative and acting like the most gigantic
idiot on earth. So what the hell, leap."

Cynthia Heimel

Push Comes to Shove
Mediation, Complaint or Due Process?
A Comparison of Conflict Resolution Procedures
Family Educational Rights and Privacy Act
Payment for Private School Placement
Manifestation Determination
Weapons and Drugs

Push Comes to Shove

I hope you will never need to use any of the information in this chapter. Every strategy and effort should be expended to avoid the need for formal conflict resolution. Special Education is the simple notion that all children should be educated to their maximum potential. I have no doubt that if children administered the law it would be a conflict-free success.

The truth is that special education has sadly become a complexity of rules, laws, customs, regulations, domains, personalities, independently elected school boards, careerists, frantic and frightened parents, domestic discord, fear of the unknown, and clashing values. Conflict is inevitable.

But if you must have conflict, try not to make it personal. Your child will be in school a long time. Waging perpetual war is not good for you or your child.

What it does to the recruitment of quality, dedicated teaching professionals is another subject entirely.

The whole point of special education is for families and professionals to work cooperatively as a team. This book has provided you with a wealth of techniques, check lists and suggestions for how to do that. Treat formal conflict resolution as a last resort. Do not go to it first and do not threaten it unless you are serious.

There is a grave danger attached here that you will permanently rupture relationships with key people in your district. What seems important today may, three years from now, not seem important enough to have institutionalized your unhappiness. Pick your battles.

Having said all that, we are parents and it is our responsibility to care for and educate our children. There are times when our vision and those of educators are far apart, and where we know, in our hearts, that our belief in the ability and future of our children is superior to theirs, and, when those circumstances are true, we have no choice but to do whatever is necessary to protect, defend and fight for our children's future. You are not a sinner if you "go after" the district.

But don't be deceived. It is a serious step.

"Last year our communication with the school was wonderful. But now it is virtually impossible. We have complained and asked for changes but nothing has happened."

"The IEP is not working. My child is sad and discouraged. The school just doesn't listen to us anymore."

"We believe a self-contained, specialized classroom would work best. The parents will not consider it and now have a lawyer who is threatening us with a due process hearing."

These are a few examples where the situation has run its course. It is now time for a formal conflict resolution to take place. What kind of resolution is available, how do they compare and which is best for you?

Mediation, Complaint or Due Process?

Mediation is an optional process. Mediation is a more formal method than a school conference or meeting, but it is less formal than a due process hearing.

A mediator, who is an impartial third party, helps parents and educators consider and develop alternatives for both sides to consider. It is an opportunity to rethink cooperation, consider new ideas, and try to compromise. But unless the parties agree, the mediator will not, and has no authority to, impose acceptance on either party. (That would be arbitration.) Since mediation is done within the parameters of special education, its goal is to ensure that the child will receive an educational program suited to his or her needs.

A Complaint to your state educational authority, typically the Department of Education, sets in motion a mandated investigation of your allegation that the school has violated federal law or regulations by failing to make or adequately implement the IEP. This resolution has the virtue of a time limit. States have rules, which vary, that require the complaint investigation to be completed within a specified period. The outside edge is usually sixty days, with many states requiring a shorter time.

Your complaint must include the facts on which your grievance is based. If the facts constitute a violation of federal law, you will prevail. In practice this means that you must demonstrate how the school's behavior has violated your child's legal right to a free and appropriate public education. That is the federal guarantee that you must show has been violated.

If the investigation upholds your complaint, a plan of corrective action will be put together and the school will have a limited amount of time, typically thirty days, to implement the plan. There are procedures in place in all states for the school to object. But since the complaint investigation is based on fact-finding, the school will most likely just comply.

Federal law and regulation require each state to develop its own procedures for complaint investigation. These written and adopted procedures must be made available to you. You can obtain them from your Director of Special Education, your principal or by contacting your state Department of Education. They all will include very specific direction on how to proceed.

A Due Process Hearing is the most formal, dreaded, and expensive method of dispute resolution. All of the federal case law interpreting IDEA is the result of appeals from Due Process Hearings. A Due Process Hearing is a federal case. The bad side of them is that they are very partisan and litigious and expensive. The good part is that they are the method by which we get the "final word" on the precise, practical meaning of the language of IDEA.

Once again, each state has slightly different procedures for handling Due Process Complaints. They are more similar than different, but you will need to follow the local rules. Basically the complaint must include your child's name and address and those of the school; a description of the nature of the problem of the child relating to the proposed changes in placement or program, including the facts you will rely on at the hearing, and a proposed resolution of the problem.

Count on your school district to be represented by a lawyer. You should be too.

These things are expensive, but if you win there are procedures by which the federal court can require the district to pay all or part of your attorney fees. Of course, if you lose you bear the total expense.

A Comparison of Three Conflict Resolution Procedures

(Remember that the details will vary from state to state)

Mediation	*Complaint Investigation*	*Due Process*
Preparation		
Agreement to mediation and selection of mediator.	District is required to respond within time period.	District retains attorney.
Gather information to investigator.	Make personnel available and prepare	Research, organize, evidence.
Mediator reviews information.	Parent submits additional information if desired.	Exchange of documents, formal "discovery."
Session, Investigation, or Hearing		
Informal discussions	Interviews and document which are confidential review gather information.	Formal. Many participants and observers.
Conference style with each side stating their position and meeting with mediator.	On-site investigation. Less formal than due process.	Litigation style, opening and closing arguments, direct and cross exam., sworn witnesses, rules of evidence, objections, etc.

Mediation	*Complaint Investigation*	*Due Process*
Negotiation and compromise, improved communication, emphasis on child and solutions.		Adversarial, polarized. Emphasis on winning.
Mediator writes agreement, ideas of parties; signature of parties.	Investigator issues a decision.	Findings of fact, conclusions of law, and a written order.
Signature indicates willingness to abide by agreement, common commitment.	Decision includes the findings, conclusions, corrective action.	Decision binding on all parties (even if they don't like it) unless reversed on appeal.
If agreement is not reached, may still pursue due process.	Can be appealed to US Dept. of Educ.	Decision can be appealed.

Attitude of the Parties

Can be friendly despite differences.	Allows evidence to be presented informally.	Cold, tense, awkward. Little tolerance for emotion. Makes future cooperation problematic.
Allows for emotion.	Less adversarial than due process.	

Mediation	*Complaint Investigation*	*Due Process*
	Expenses	
Few hours preparation and a day for mediation.	Staff time to prepare materials, on-site visit, etc.	50 to 100 hours attorney time and several day trial.
Money: Time lost from work, transportation, mediation fee.	Money: Time lost from work, hiring sub. fees, attorneys,	Time lost from work, pay witness transcript, etc.

Obviously each of these methods has their virtue. Review their requirements and likely disposition before choosing one over the other. I would not compromise one iota our right to a due process hearing. After all, federal law guarantees our children's educational rights, and access to federal court is our enforcement mechanism. But due process hearings are a serious, emotional, and financial gamble as well as running the risk of opening wounds that may harm your child down the road.

Family Educational Rights and Privacy Act (FERPA)

Another potential source of conflict has to do with personal information the school will have in its files concerning your child and your family. Many people would prefer that no one knows their child is receiving special education. This law is designed to protect the privacy of your child's educational records. The law applies to all schools that receive funds from the US Department of Education. That would be virtually every public school in the USA.

FERPA gives you certain rights. Those rights, like others, transfer to your child on their eighteenth birthday or are attending school beyond the high school level. Students and former students to whom these rights apply are called eligible students.

Parents or eligible students have the right to inspect and review all of the school's education records. Schools are not required to provide copies of materials unless, for reasons such as distance, it is impossible for parents or eligible students to inspect the records personally. If you wish to have copies made the school is free to charge you a copying fee.

Parents or eligible students have the right to request that a school correct records that are inaccurate or misleading. If the school decides not to accept that their records are flawed, the parent or eligible student has the right to a formal hearing. After the hearing, if the school still refuses to amend its records, the parent or eligible student has the right to place a written statement in the record setting out why they believe the information to be flawed. That statement remains part of the permanent record.

Generally the school must have written permission from the parent or the eligible student before releasing any portion of information about the student's school records. However, the law allows schools to disclose records, without consent, to the following parties:
- School employees who have a valid educational need.
- Other schools to which a student is transferring.
- Law enforcement.
- Appropriate parties in connection with financial aid.
- Organizations doing certain studies for the school.

Payment for Private School Placement

Under certain circumstances you may place your child in a private school and bill your school district for the cost. However, this circumstance is limited and requires a lot of steps before it becomes reality.

IEP teams have the authority to place a student in the appropriate placement, including private schools. If they do that, the district is responsible for cost. Obviously districts do not want to ever do that, since it is not only expensive but may also be seen as an admission that their programs are not adequate.

Our discussion here applies only to situations where parents place their child in a private school without the consent or referral of a public school.

If a due process hearing officer or federal judge determines that the child was not provided with a free and appropriate public education, the law allows placement of the child in a private school with costs borne by the public school. However, payment of those costs may be denied or reduced if parents did not first give notice to the school district of their intention to place their child in a private school. That notice must include all of the following information:

- A clear statement that the parents are rejecting the school district placement.
- A statement of the parent's concerns.
- A statement of the parent's intention to enroll their child in a private school at public expense.

Notice can be given in two ways, as long as the notice includes the information given above.

- Verbal notice at the most recent IEP meeting prior to the removal of the child from public school; or
- Written notice ten business days prior to the removal of the child from public school.

There are exceptions to the notice provision, exception is allowed, for example, if the parent is illiterate or cannot write English. In addition, other factors may affect reimbursement of private school expense. An example being a situation where parents do not make their child available to the school district for evaluation.

Discipline

Parents know better than anyone that children with disabilities may exhibit some pretty odd behavior. In many cases the behavior has the potential to be disruptive of a classroom or frightening to others who do not understand it. The most-knee jerk reaction that schools and others can embrace is to exclude students with disabilities because of their behavior. To some observers, typically teacher's unions, administrators, and people who are ignorant of the subject, this approach has a superficial appeal. But here is the dilemma, the one fact you need to understand in order to handle the whole arena of discipline for children in special education.

Federal law guarantees a free and appropriate public education to every child eligible for special education. That right cannot be reality if, for example, a child with autism behaves autistically and can be expelled for behavior directly related to his or her disability. You cannot have it both ways. Either there is no right to a free and appropriate public education (since children with disabilities can be expelled for exhibiting behavior consistent with their disability) or the school must learn how to deal with behaviors and make distinctions between those that are related to the disability and those that are not. This process of distinction is known as a "manifestation determination." In other words, is the behavior a manifestation of the disability or is it not?

If the behavior "manifested" is not disability related the child may be disciplined or expelled the same as any other child. If the behavior is disability related, there are some specific differences in consequence that you should be aware of.

Manifestation Determination

The IEP team does the manifestation determination. The team is required to consider all information based on the individual and not on the category of his or her disability.

The information the IEP team may consider will include evaluations, including functional behavioral assessments, information from parents, friends, and family members, school observation of the student and all relevant IEP placement information.

When looking at the student's misbehavior, the first question to ask is whether or not the IEP and placement were appropriate in the first place. Was the placement responsive to behavioral, social, and emotional needs of the student that impact his or her educational performance? Was the student receiving reasonable educational benefit from the IEP before the misconduct?

The next inquiry should be to look at the misbehavior and ask whether the special education services, supplementary aids and services, and behavioral intervention strategies implemented were consistent with the IEP. In other words, were the required services implemented in good faith or was the student being set up for failure?

Also ask the team to address whether or not the student's ability to understand the impact and consequences of behavior was impacted by their disability. The IEP team is required to take into account the totality of circumstance including the child's cognitive capacity and the specific facts surrounding the misconduct.

The ultimate question to be answered is whether or not the child's disability impaired their ability to control their behavior. Was the behavior impulsive rather than intentional?

If the team determines that the behavior manifested was disability related your child will enjoy some procedural protections that come along with special education eligibility. If not, they can be dealt with like anyone else.

Weapons and Drugs

Once again, it is important to remember that specific details may vary slightly from state to state. I am not giving you legal advice. What appears in this book is an overview of law and procedures and a warning to you as to your rights. It is your responsibility to find and follow your local requirements.

One of the most outrageous misstatements that have been made in recent years about students with disabilities has to do with their alleged right to attend school with weapons and illegal drugs and that the law prevents schools from taking any action. That is preposterous, untrue, and not helpful. Children who are found in possession of weapons or controlled substances can be removed from the school and placed in an alternative educational setting, that is, one where they can be monitored and their safety and that of other students assured.

If the student is found in possession of weapons or drugs, the IEP team will decide on the appropriate educational setting. Before this can happen, the school must notify the parents about its decision to pursue disciplinary action and enclose a written notice of procedural safeguards. The IEP Team must meet and make a manifestation determination within a specified amount of time, typically ten days.

Services must continue to be provided in both a special education and regular education format but not necessarily in the old placement. If there is no functional behavioral assessment in place, the IEP team must convene and develop one. If there is one, it must be reviewed or revised.

The IEP team must give parents prior written notice of its intent to make a change in the child's placement. The child may be removed and placed in an alternative educational setting for up to forty-five days. The district, at its discretion, may ask for extensions beyond forty-five days.

A "weapon" is a weapon if it is a firearm (including a starter gun), the frame of a weapon, a silencer, or any destructive device, such as a grenade, gas bomb, rocket, etc.

A "dangerous weapon" is typically defined as something that can be used under certain circumstances to cause death or serious bodily injury. A "deadly weapon," on the other hand, is one specifically designed to cause death or serious bodily injury.

A weapon is considered covered by IDEA if the student brings it to school or a school function, or the student acquires it at school.

School district personnel are required to report crimes committed by students with disabilities the same as they would with any other student. Naturally students in special education enjoy the procedural rights and safeguards enjoyed by any other person who is accused of crime.

If a child in special education is charged with a crime, must the school provide special education and disciplinary records to "appropriate authorities" when it reports the crime? The answer is yes, but only as allowed by FERPA. The records may be turned over if the parents give their written consent, if the school has been served with a proper court order or subpoena, or there is a health or safety emergency. If you live in a state that has a statute creating an information-sharing system that protects against these disclosures, the school may be prohibited from turning them over.

Is There a Change of Placement?

Once the IEP team has made an educational placement only the IEP team can change it. There are significant procedural safeguards against whimsical or arbitrary change. There are some discipline situations that constitute a change of placement. In other situations they do not.

Generally the following circumstances do not constitute a change of placement and thus the procedural rules do not apply.

If the child is removed for up to ten days, the parents must be given written notice and the school is not required to provide services. If the removal period exceeds ten days, services must be provided and the school personnel may decide which services are provided and where.

Removals for up to ten days do not require a functional behavioral assessment. If the period is longer than ten days, one must be made and a behavioral intervention plan put in place; the IEP team must meet in order to consider those revisions.

Removals that do constitute a change of placement are generally only those that exceed ten days. The school's first obligation is to provide parents with a written notice of intent to proceed with some intended action, such as suspension or expulsion hearing. The notice must contain procedural safeguards.

These removals require a manifestation determination. The school can only proceed with a regular disciplinary removal if the IEP team finds that the behavior was NOT a manifestation of the child's disability. If the misconduct is a manifestation, then it must be addressed through the IEP/placement process.

Congress, parents and professionals have gone back and forth on "discipline and removal." The 2005 amendments to IDEA include the latest attempts to codify it. The details vary. Personalities play a large part and, obviously, the best remedy is to have in place a well-implemented IEP that includes strategies for behavioral interventions.

But the dilemma remains that the nation cannot provide a free and appropriate education guarantee for all students, while excluding children whose disability manifests itself in alienating behavior. Your job as a parent advocate is to develop and assure implementation of the IEP. If your child misbehaves in a way that drives a district to pursue formal disciplinary action, your best defense is the manifestation determination.

The bottom line is that we parents have the responsibility of educating others about our child's needs and oddities. Mostly our kids are not a danger to anyone. Sometimes they are. Discipline and removal, like dispute resolution, is a sad road to pursue. A wise parent anticipates as much as possible destructive episodes in the life of their child and takes steps to intervene before it blows up into an unmanageable situation.

Chapter 8

THE FUTURE OF SPECIAL EDUCATION

"The important thing is not to stop questioning. Curiosity has its own reason for existing. One cannot help but be in awe when he contemplates the mysteries of eternity, of life, of the marvelous structure of reality. It is enough if one tries merely to comprehend a little of this mystery every day. Never lose a holy curiosity."

Albert Einstein

Who Added "Special?"
A Normal and Natural Part of the Human Condition
Backlash
Where Does the Money Come From?
Diversity
Some Ironies of Our Success
Toward Abolition of Special Education
A Well Earned Place

Who Added "Special?"

IDEA is the simple concept that all children go to school. Furthermore, they get to go to school close to home with children who are their neighbors. That seems simple enough. But educators, faced with a new obligation, namely, to educate all children, found the paradigm so shocking as to require a new name. In a gesture both whimsical and prophetic, it was decided that the new reality would be labeled "special."

"Special," according to the American Heritage Dictionary means, "surpassing what is common or usual." Who, then, are these students who are "special?" Who are the ones who "surpass what is common or usual"?

Roget's Thesaurus, 6th Edition, answers those questions for us. "Special Education Student" is defined as one who is "learning disabled or impaired; slow learner; underachiever; handicapped or retarded; emotionally disturbed or culturally challenged." In this context, "special" takes on a dictionary meaning quite opposite of what IDEA purports to promote. If IDEA stands for the proposition that all children enjoy an equal right to a free and appropriate public education, that concept is immediately undercut by the adoption of a label for those who go beyond "what is common or usual."

To follow that thought, let's look at the definition of another word, "pretty." According to the same dictionary "pretty" means "attractive in a pleasing or delicate way." But "pretty good" actually means not so good. Thus we are victimized by what is intended being perverted by what is actually meant.

In our case, "special" turns out to mean something nearer to "eccentric," "contrived," or, recently, "expensive." It is emphatically not something that is common or usual.

What a wonderful game this is for linguists to play. What a nightmare for children and parents who have to live with it. Lurking beneath the sugary, surface façade of normalcy is the unspoken but accepted truth that "those kids" are actually an experiment. A sort of well intended, but, perhaps, transitory good deed that "we" are doing for "them."

What is it about America that requires labeling? What is wrong with referring to all of this as simply "education." While many of us loathe the idea that our child is in "special" education, we must remember that there are thousands of families who desperately want their child to be there. It is their only access to specialized instruction to address the unique learning needs of their child. The very specific eligibility requirements for special education prevent many children from ever accessing curriculum that is designed just for them. Curriculum that will maximize their learning potential.

This trait, of making everything label-tidy, serves to make the opposite truer. Children should not be required to meet some arbitrary standard in order to access an educational curriculum that is designed to meet their needs. Children who do meet the criteria should not be labeled "special." By insisting on this label, we single out children with disabilities, treat them differently and think about their educational needs as something different from the educational needs of "normal" children. In fact, they are the same.

A Normal and Natural Part of the Human Condition

Ironically, the assigning of the designation of "special" to our kids betrays both the philosophy of IDEA and the fact that disability is just a normal and natural part of the human condition.

As a young man I lived in Paris in a cheap, walk-up, cold-water apartment not far from the Louver. In those days the museum was free on Thursday's and I used to go there for the warmth, among other things. After Eleanor was born I recalled a small, soapstone carving dating from 2,500 BCE in the Mesopotamian Section. In my memory there was something very familiar about that piece and I was anxious to return and see if it was what I remembered.

When I did return I discovered that my suspicion was true. There, on the shelf, is a small rendering in soapstone. Unmistakably, a young girl with Down syndrome. But it is more than that. It is so delicately and lovingly rendered as to only have been done by an artisan who loved this girl very much. Perhaps a parent, or another relative. Resounding down through the centuries is a face that evokes the primordial love that we all have for our children. A lesson sent down to me by an artist long dead and forgotten.

The lesson I learned is that disability has been around a long time. Your child is not an aberration. When we resort to prenatal screenings and termination of pregnancies of fetuses with a condition we currently regard as undesirable, we are messing with some strong human forces. People with disabilities have been around as long as there have been humans. That has not changed. What have changed are how people are treated, how their humanity is recognized, and our collective expectation of how they will live. But disability is not an accident or a curse. It is a normal part of life.

Backlash

The educational reform agenda codified in IDEA is a model for all kinds of social service and planning. The mere concept of an Individual Plan is revolutionary. IDEA introduced and demonstrates that such individual attention is precisely what people with disabilities require.

Today adult services for are moving toward person-centered-planning. The use of techniques such a "mapping" helps find an individual plan to help each person achieve his or her goals. Many of these plans are called "Individual Service Plans" and owe their acceptance to IDEA.

Recently the National Disability Rights Network was awarded grant money to locate and help people with disabilities who have been displaced by Hurricane Katrina. Once these people are located the vehicle to help put their lives back together will be called an IRP, an Individual Recovery Plan. The influence of IDEA's progressive thinking can be found in many places.

By any objective measurement, the law is a grand success. Each of us has a story to contradict that statement. But in the big picture, the right of every child to a free and appropriate public education is little short of revolutionary. And, like other big changes from how things are remembered to have been during the "good old days," the education of children with disabilities has provoked a reactionary body of thinking.

This backlash against students with disabilities and IDEA is mostly spoken of as an issue of money and budgets. But, make no mistake, beneath that respectable front lies prejudice, a belief that it is simply "not worth it" to educate our kids and an even darker sense that "normal" kids might catch something. Our children are different and therefore unsightly in some eyes. Adults of today have no memory of going to school with peers with disabilities. Somehow it just doesn't seem right to them. We are tolerated and patted on the head. But the toleration is tinged with skepticism and suspicion, and, it is not an exaggeration to say, a longing to be done with us.

Take every opportunity to participate in "normal" school activity. Volunteer as a driver or chaperone for field trips. Serve on volunteer councils and PTAs. If we withdraw into our own little communities, we are reinforcing stereotypes. "They belong with their own kind," is what got our children into institutions in the first place. Our biggest weapon is a belief in our children. If you demonstrate through your own demeanor that you believe your child is a regular, normal, and natural human being, that message will be heard. It's up to you to convey your expectations.

The most "respectable" part of this backlash has to do with the cost of special education. Understanding how this is financed is an important part of your advocacy obligation.

Where Does the Money Come From?

Obviously public schools are financed with public money. As educational costs rise, people become concerned about where the money comes from and how it is spent. Many states and local communities have seen tax-based revenues decrease in recent years. More and more the political arena is full of ideas about how to best educate America's children while at the same time containing costs. Sadly, students in special education are frequently pointed to as somehow causing the low level of achievement, supplies, and teacher training that plague many communities. The temptation to say, "If it weren't for those kids" there would be plenty of money for normal education is strong. And we hear it spoken more and more.

The first funding track for special education is the "federal contribution."

IDEA itself is based on money. Any federal law must have some basis for federal jurisdiction. Schools that accept federal money are required to follow the provisions of IDEA. Since the federal government is so involved in so many areas of educational funding that, in practice, means that every public school must abide by IDEA.

As a federal law, IDEA was enacted by the Congress of the United States. From the first discussion, members of Congress were aware that there would be additional educational costs associated with special education. Originally the plan was for the federal government to assume those costs. It has never happened.

Congressional money appropriation is a different procedure than the adoption of laws. In other words, IDEA was adopted as law but no money was appropriated to send to the states. A separate procedure to add money does happen, as part of the budget setting process, and it is called "the federal contribution." Unfortunately it has never come close to full funding.

The "federal contribution" has grown over the years and is now higher than it has ever been. It is simply a sum of money that goes to the states based on how many children they have enrolled in special education. Right now it is less that $1,000/student, but it is money must be spent on special education. It cannot be commingled with state general fund money.

The second funding track is a formula used by the states for paying for their schools. In some communities local school boards have taxing authority. Generally this tax is imposed on real property and sometimes on income. Out of this tax revenue schools are funded. In other states education costs are paid by state government, which doles out money to local districts according to their specified formula.

A common formula for funding special education is called the "2X." In its simplest form you simply add up the number of children enrolled in the district (the kid count) and divide that number into the total amount of educational dollars available and the schools gets so much per child. Since students in special education have specially designed curriculum with supplemental aids and supports there are more expenses associated with it. To address this the "2X" formula doubles the cost per child on an IEP. The result is that the district gets twice as much money for a child in special education as they do for those who are not.

This fact has caused a lot of misinformation to circulate about special education. Parents learn these formulas and deduce that their child is, therefore, entitled to an educational plan whose expense equals the formula plus the federal contribution. This is NOT true. Your child is entitled to whatever it costs to implement their IEP. The dollar amount is not attached to a child.

Because special education generates twice as much money for the school many educators and other parents see that as a drain on regular education. However, this extra money goes to the school district and not just to special education. It is based on the belief that special education cannot be stronger than the school that supports it. That a local school can spend extra-generated revenue any way it chooses. Not only is that money not earmarked just for your child, it is not even reserved for special education.

As a cost containment measure, there is a cap on special education eligibility. Generally schools cannot find more than 11 per cent of their enrollees eligible. That, of course, makes no sense. Should we not be moving in the direction of providing whatever educational services children need without relying on arbitrary numbers?

An open question is whether schools spend more money on special education than they take in. Although there are plenty of children with serious disabilities who require expensive services, they represent a tiny percentage of all children eligible for special education.

Imagine a child who needs a one-on-one educational assistant, toileting help, respirator, wheel chair, and assistive technology. These things are provided by IDEA in order to honor the Free and Appropriate Public Education requirement.

Clearly that child is costing more than that child is bringing in.

But for every child with that level of need there are many times more eligible children whose sole special education service is thirty minutes a month of teacher consultation time with a specialist. If you wish to be vulgar enough to reduce education to money, it is clear that the district is "making" money on those special education students. The theory, which mostly works, is that it all levels out over a large district.

For small school districts that have a student with involved and serious disabilities that outstrip the school's resources, states have back-up agencies such as Educational Service Districts or Regional Programs. These agencies provide the related services personnel and their expertise that small schools cannot afford to maintain on their own.

Special education is funded through a combination of the "federal contribution" and state funding formula. By understanding the basics of where the money comes from, you are better able to counter criticism of the cost of special education. If there is a blame to be ascribed, it is on members of Congress who have voted for the substance of IDEA but have consistently failed to live up to their promise of full federal funding.

The bottom line on funding is that you are not entitled to a set dollar amount for your child. The IEP team makes the decision as to services necessary to make reasonable educational progress and the funding follows the services. Emphasis is on the individual. Funding follows the student. Students do not follow the funding.

Additionally, many states now have "high cost" laws which reimburse school districts for the cost of low incidence high cost students. It is simply not true that special education is some kind of budget breaker that impacts the educational rights of other students.

"Maintenance of effort" refers to a federal rule, which purports to forbid special education funding from being reduced by local or state educational agencies. It has been interpreted in a way that makes it a pretty hollow threat for advocates attempting to maintain funding. It does, however, exist, and you can find the details of your state's rule by asking your Department of Education. This is not a great weapon but it does no harm to bring it up.

Overcrowding, old facilities, and teacher grievances are not caused by you or by special education. The law guarantees your child the service he or she needs to succeed. That is your top priority. But that does not mean that school issues are not your problem. Work to correct deficiencies in education. But do not accept the blame for them. Schools are not schools unless are children are welcomed and embraced. Blaming minorities of any kind is a cheap way of finding an excuse for professional shortcomings.

"Diversity"

With the arrival of more and more students from diverse cultural and ethnic backgrounds, American education has been forced to make some changes in how it treats these children. The role of "melting pot" continues to be an important one but just how this will happen is the subject of great public and political debate.

One thing we know for sure is that "diversity" has become an important mantra. Diversity recognizes that every child is unique. It recognizes that everyone has value, a point of view, and a contribution to make. If that sounds familiar it is because those principles have been lifted right out of special education law.

The educational benefit of going to school with children from wide racial, religious, cultural, and economic backgrounds is well documented. Indeed, in the absence of a military draft, public school is now called upon to play a role similar to that of universal military service. That is to expose and remind a huge range of citizens that they have a great stake in this nation's welfare. It gives people an opportunity to know and work with others who are normally not within their circle of acquaintance. Public schools have a huge role to play in perpetuating democracy.

Too often we overlook the fact that our kids, too, are simply part of the diversity pot.

There will be few opportunities in life for "normal" people to interact so closely with people with disabilities. Rather than passively accept the label of "different," change the subject to "diversity" and claim your rightful place on the continuum of experience and challenge that is modern education.

Special education students are not guests. Nor are they simply to be tolerated and indulged. We belong in school and in every other corner of American life. Our children have great contributions to make to this world. Help others to appreciate how lucky they are to have the opportunity to glimpse life through a challenging lens. Others grow enormously from this chance. Be proud of your kids. They are strong, smart, and a part of life. They are "normal."

Some Ironies of Our Success

Parents created special education. We all owe a debt for the work that (mostly) mothers did in creating educational opportunity for all of us. The educational reform agenda that has been adopted over the past half-century came about because parents like us learned to organize themselves politically and hit the right nerve with policy makers and politicians.

Nothing about a free and appropriate public education was handed to us. There was not a day when the educational establishment reached out and invited us into their schools. We got there by hard work, vision, and a belief that education is the key to success for all children.

Because of parent advocacy there are now budgets, staff, bureaucracies, and specialists whose function is presumably to work together with families to assure educational success. The child's needs are the focal point of the whole educational reform agenda. But keeping the child in the center of the picture has become increasingly difficult with the rise of a formal structure, which, inevitably, morphs, into a system that appears to serve itself first and the child as an afterthought.

Early history of disability advocacy is largely a struggle with bureaucracy. Ironically, as we became more successful, our effort contributed to the creation of a truly Byzantine bureaucracy. One that has the potential to overwhelm the simple concepts of fairness and hope, which we codified in modern law.

Bureaucracy is, by definition, a narrow and inward looking thing. Bureaucracies have a long and tragic history of learning how to perpetuate and replicate themselves while subordinating, and even scoffing, at their founding principles such as "justice," "freedom," and "independence." Those terms become hard for bureaucrats to define. And it is precision that they thrive on.

In the beginning, when it was just "the moms and kids," there were no services and there were no bureaucracies. For a while there was the moms, kids, and a few dedicated and visionary professionals, but little bureaucracy. The good administrators and professionals did what we told them and the bad ones didn't do much of anything. The more the parents, now advocates, fought, the more the system responded and, low and behold, whole federal, state and local agencies were created. Today they exist, not so much to serve, as to oversee, manage, evaluate, and monitor.

For people working within that structure this meant going from having a job to do to having a career to protect. Careerists started speaking on behalf of us all, steering us in one direction or another and always, always, keeping their jobs and prestige no matter the outcome for children. It makes me feel, cynically, that when asked what I think Eleanor's role is all this is, I can reply, "raw material to fuel the disability business." Not a healthy or happy thought. But, sadly, more true than the founding mothers of IDEA would have imagined.

Today it is the bureaucracies that control budgets and issue edicts. We created these agencies with our blood, sweat, and tears. Often they act as if special education was all about them and that they know more than we do. That is an arrogance of power, which disheartens us, and threatens the dream of IDEA.

Because of teacher contracts, unions, organization, and bureaucracy, some school people are well aware that all they have to do to survive is wait until you and your child age out of their school. They know they will be there long after you are gone. This is never what was intended. This reform agenda was created to empower people with disabilities and their families. It was not created to fuel a cottage industry. The system's loyalty needs to always focus on needs of the child first. Don't shirk an opportunity to make that point.

This irony can be understood better, by looking at the use of the term "retarded." One of the most hurtful, and one of the most common, schoolyard insults is to label someone a "retard." If there is one thing that self-advocacy organizations have promoted, it is the realization that the old mantra "sticks and stones may break my bones, but words will never hurt me," is as false as can be. Words do hurt. If you doubt that, take a look at the face of your child the first time someone uses that insult on him or her. For us, the use of that word is simply gratuitous cruelty. It means nothing except labeling and humiliation.

But for way too many researchers, employees of University Centers for Excellence, Governor's Planning Councils, psychologists, and graduate students, the word "retardation" has taken on a holy mantra. According to them it is not an epithet but science. The need to do "research," and to apply "scientific" principles in the study of our children, is not only of interest to them, but is essential if they are to maintain their privileged place in the hierarchy.

Thus, a simple principle, such as the right to dignity and education, which was the message of the parent founders of IDEA, becomes suborned and trivialized in the face of "objective" research. Our children are human beings. They are not guinea pigs. And, more to the point, they are not lab rats.

When the ambition of a career becomes the highest purpose of public policy work, and when the ameliorative role of families is held in contempt, the staffing of regulatory agencies with people hostile to our objectives, results in the horse following behind the cart. Keep your eyes open for that. It is more and more common and its proximity to-out and-out corruption is apparent.

There is nothing wrong with you spending your precious time and energy on "official" advocacy organizations. But it is a wise parent who evaluates just whose interests that agency is actually serving.

The mothers who created IDEA affiliated themselves with the Arc in large numbers. As their children aged, their attention was turned to adult services and one of the most popular "services" was the creation of what are now called "sheltered workshops." These are typically non-profit corporations who benefit from waivers in a state's minimum wage laws. When there were no services, just having a place to send your adult child during the day was a positive that people did not question. Today, most of us are not thrilled with an employment "opportunity" that pays pennies-per-hour. Sheltered workshops are not a place for independence and pride. Yet, ironically, many of the same Arc chapters that gave us IDEA, are still financially dependent on the profits from their sponsored workshops.

In September 2005 over 2,000 delegates came to Washington, DC to participate in "The Alliance for Full Participation." That was a summit meeting of professionals, bureaucrats, functionaries, careerists, and parents to discuss and vote on issues regarding developmental disabilities. When it came to the question of sheltered workshops, the delegates were asked if it was time to close them. Their choices were "yes" and "not yet." In other words no one was required to actually vote to keep them open. Nor was anyone charged with closing them. The operators of these sweat shops were allowed to maintain their political correctness while still reaping profit from their own operations. Another irony, where the facts of life contradict founding principles, and even consistency of thought and deed.

In my own state of Oregon, 200,000 poor and disabled people have lost their Oregon Health Plan coverage during the past two years. There are now enormous wait lists just to get a referral to an adult service brokerage. Direct care workers wages are frozen, staff turnover threatens the very stability of the service system, there are virtually no crisis intervention services, and, yet, the "official" advocacy agencies have all examined their strategic plans and declared themselves a success. If they reached a different conclusion they would risk losing their federal funding.

Just how one disaster after another can add up to success, is a result that can only be reached by ignoring the needs of people with disabilities, and evaluating yourself based on the number of emails you send out in a year. If their self-evaluation had to do with the impact on the lives of people with disabilities, and not their adopted goals, there could be no evaluation that labeled their efforts successful. For them, a good year is one in which no staff are laid off and the budget is not cut. Who is being served? Not me. Not Eleanor. Not people with disabilities.

These ironies are a fact of life. We have to learn to live with them. But, keep your eye on the prize. Your child was not placed on this earth to provide anybody with a career opportunity. Your children are here to enjoy the best life they possibly can. Objectifying them, and dismissing our natural concerns for their welfare, is neither professional nor visionary, and will lead nowhere.

There is a role for professionals and research. But that role is not to dehumanize anybody. We created this field of "special" education. We thought it up, we fought to make it a reality, and we are in danger of having the whole thing taken over by soulless "systems." Special Education is about passion. It is about doing what's right. We will work with and respect others. But never lose sight of the fact that this system belongs to us. It is here to serve us. We have the right to expect more than being the object of someone's curiosity.

Having a child with a disability gives you a presence and credibility that will never be approached by some career seeker who got his or her start while volunteering at a bingo game. Our children are not "interesting." They are just human beings that deserve something better than being a funding source for a new generation of oppressors.

Curious, isn't it, that people who had been "have nots," as they slowly work their way up the social ladder, are unable to take their values along. Too often they simply adopt the values we wish they would replace. It is as if there is some kind of mandated role that former revolutionaries (I believe the current label is "change agents") feel obligated to adopt when it comes to be their turn in the drivers' seat. As Bob Dylan said of them, "don't follow leaders…and watch the parking meters."

Or, to quote another venerable rock and roll philosophy, this one from The Who, "See the new boss, just like the old boss." We have the right to expect more. And, certainly, our children have the right to expect a lot more!

Toward Abolition of Special Education

The frustrations many of us feel with special education can obscure the truth of its success. The fact that it exists at all is a minor miracle and a testament to the power of dreaming. The sole political capital that parents had to expend in the political process was simple justice. There is nothing very sophisticated about it. Just an easy to understand, person-centered, scheme that grants the right to a free and appropriate public education to everyone.

That simplicity is its own genius. Imagine the things that special education stands for. An individually created learning program that is designed to meet the unique learning style of every child. Measurable goals and outcomes. A requirement for regular review to see if it is working. The provision of aids and services to assist in reaching educational goals. Teacher training, family empowerment and the opportunity to work in harmony with a team to do what's best for one child at a time.

Why then are these progressive notions limited to people with disabilities? Would we not all be better served if every child could benefit from the educational principals of IDEIA? Would we not all be better off without the label of "special?"

Throughout American social services there is an implicit separation. There are those who "need" and those who "give." People with disabilities are given "services" (if they are lucky). We talk openly of people with "special needs." But are those needs so special? Would we not be a better nation and a better people if the concepts of IDEA were extended to the population as a whole? Are we not better off considering the needs of humanity rather than the needs of the disabled?

We all need to think bigger. Pigeonholing people according to categories and labels is no way to run the world. It creates elites, hierarchies, and the opportunity for abuse.

Leaders tell us to "think outside the box." But, what I observe is that these same leaders have adopted the language of the people they wish to supplant. We won't make change if all we offer is the same; the same style, the same reproaches and the same paradigm. If we cannot move beyond the normal ways of imposing belief and restraining the recalcitrant to toe the line, if we are simply inspired by people presently in power and all we wish to do is replace them, aren't we, at bottom, the same danger?

Let us call, instead, for the abolition of "special" education and realize that all children are entitled to the same thing because they, and their needs, are, mostly, the same. Perpetuating differences through arcane evaluations and labels is not progress. The 21st Century is a good place to start recognizing that we are all in this together. We cannot afford separateness.

And to those who will say that we cannot afford the expense of extending individual curriculum to every student I say we can. There is not now and never has been a shortage of money. The issue is where the ample supply of money is being spent. What is lacking is the political will to change priorities and spend the money where it will do the most good. If education is America's number one priority then it should be funded to the extent necessary to maximize each student's potential.

Today a baby born in the United States has less chance of living until their first birthday than one born in Slovakia. That fact gives us all something to think about. Just where are the priorities? And who is addressing them? Whose interests are being served? Where do the futures of our children fit into these plans? What can we do about it?

A Well-Earned Place

It is time for people with disabilities to assume responsibility as complete citizens. We cannot just be asking for things. We need to offer things as well.

The tax system of your state and nation is a disability issue. War and peace is a disability issue as is global warming. I have said repeatedly that belief in your child is your best tool. Your child is more than a person with a disability. Encourage them to think that way. Seize every opportunity to grab full citizenship. Teach your children to be responsible people and to think of themselves as leaders and contributors. Make them the leaders of tomorrow.

Franklin Delano Roosevelt lead the United States through some of the most perilous times in its history while using a wheelchair. We all have an obligation to see to it that the next time a person with a disability becomes President of the United States there will be no need for them to hide their disability. It can be a mark of strength and pride, as it should be.

Let us turn our thoughts to what we can do to make this a fairer and more just nation for everyone. Where are our priorities? What can you do to make them more humane?

Justin Dart, Jr., recipient of the Presidential Medal of Freedom, wheel chair user, and regarded as the father of the Americans with Disabilities Act, left behind a dying declaration that can guide us all into an inclusive and rich future. On his deathbed he postulated questions and challenges that we need to hear everyday.

I want to end this book with his words. As he said so well, "listen to the heart of this old soldier."

"I adamantly protest the richest culture in the history of the world which still incarcerates millions of humans with and without disabilities in barbaric institutions, backrooms and worse, windowless cells or oppressive perceptions, for the lack of the most elementary empowerment supports."

"I do so love all the patriots of this and every nation who have fought and sacrificed to bring us to the threshold of this beautiful human dream. I do so love America the beautiful and our wild, creative, beautiful people. I do so love you, my beautiful colleagues in the disability and civil rights movement."

Life, of course, goes on in all of its archaic splendor and rich irony. While I am finishing this book, Eleanor is approaching her eighteenth birthday. And for a person with a disability that is an important demarcation. It is time for her adult labeling ritual. Just being born with Down syndrome is not enough. She has been required to go through a meaningless and expensive "evaluation" to determine her eligibility for adult services.

At the same time, she goes about her business of being a high school student with high expectations for her own future. This term she is taking an English Literature class in a regular classroom.

During the same recent week she was officially labeled as a person with "mild mental retardation" and received an A in her English class! Like all people with disabilities in America she is caught between two versions of "official" truth. One of them is wrong.

How do we know what is true?

Are we real citizens or are we an expensive luxury to be indulged during times of prosperity and shunned during times of want? Are we human beings entitled to dignity and respect or are we perpetual children always needing protection and supervision? Can we accept that risk is part of life and that no one can be totally safe?

IDEIA has given us a window of opportunity. Like Eleanor's tribal labeling ceremony and her academic success, the dream and the reality don't always make sense.

Whether or not this dream becomes a reality for every American is a question that will be answered by our children when they become adults. All we can do is support them now.

It remains for us to bequeath to them the words of Justin Dart, Jr., "Lead on!"

But, it remains for them to decide the future.

Glossary

Acronyms and Common Jargon

Acronym: A word formed from the first or first few letters of several words, e.g. SSI (Supplemental Security Income).

Acronyms are merely a shorthand method of talking. They are commonly used by people to simplify communication. For those of us not "in the loop," acronyms have no meaning. Attending a meeting where others are speaking in acronyms can cut you out of the conversation faster than anything.

To be a real participant at your child's educational meetings you must understand what is being said. If people are using acronyms that you do not understand ask them to stop! If written material contains acronyms the problem is equally acute.

The best thing to do is to ask that they not be used. But, they are a handy shortcut and we all fall into the habit of using them. If they are used insist they their meaning be explained.

As you gain more experience you too will probably start using them.

Remember, the bottom line here is that you have the right to know precisely what is happening!!

Here is a list of common acronyms used by special education professionals, advocates and social service agencies. The list is incomplete. You should learn and keep track of acronyms commonly used in your state or community.

AFS	Adult and Family Services
AFC	Adult Foster Care
ADD	Attention Deficit Disorder
ADD #2	Administration on Developmental Disabilities
A & D	Alcohol and Drug
ADA	Americans with Disabilities Act
AG	Attorney General
AR	Administrative Rules
AT	Assistive Technology
BP	Benefits Planning
CM	Case Management
CP	Cerebral Palsy
CFR	Code of Federal Regulations
CMHP	Community Mental Health Program
CMS	Center for Medicaid Services
CQI	Continuous Quality Improvement
DOE	Department of Education
DHR	Department of Human Resources
DOJ	Department of Justice
DD	Developmental Disability
DSO	Disability Service Office
EI	Early Intervention
ECSE	Early Childhood Special Education
ESD	Educational Service District
EMT	Emergency Medical Technician
FAPE	Free and Appropriate Public Education
FAS	Fetal Alcohol Syndrome
FERPA	Family Education Rights Privacy Act
FP	Future Planning
FY	Fiscal Year
GF	General Fund
GAP	Guardianship, Advocacy and Planning
HAVA	Help America Vote Act
HMO	Health Maintenance Organization
HB	House Bill

ILC	Independent Living Center
ICC	Interagency Coordinating Council
IDEA	Individuals with Disabilities Education Act
IDEIA	Individuals with Disabilities Education Improvement Act – refers to IDEA after 2004 Amendments
IEP	Individual Education Program
IFSP	Individual Family Support Plan
ICFMR	Intermediate Care Facility for the Mentally Retarded
IRS	Internal Revenue Service
LEA	Local Education Administration
LRE	Least Restrictive Environment
LRP	Long Range Plan
MR	Mental Retardation
NAMI	National Alliance of the Mentally Ill
NDRN	National Disability Rights Network
OT	Occupational Therapy
P & A	Protection and Advocacy
PLOP	Present Level of Performance
PFP	Personal Futures Planning
PTIC	Parent Training and Information Center
PT	Physical Therapy
QA	Quality Assurance
RCH	Residential Care Home
RFP	Request for Proposal
RFQP	Request for Qualified Providers
SABE	Self Advocates Becoming Empowered
SB	Senate Bill
SILP	Semi-Independent Living Program
SED	Severely Emotionally Disturbed
STP	Specialized Training Program
SSA	Social Security Administration
SA	Self Advocate
SSI	Supplemental Security Income
SEMP	Supported Employment Program
TR	Teaching Research

TQM	Total Quality Management
UCP	United Cerebral Palsy
USDOE	United States Department of Education
VR	Vocational Rehabilitation
WAC	Work Activity Center

Appendix

Eleanor was in fourth grade before she realized there was such a thing as a self-contained classroom. She wrote, with my help, this article while attending a conference in Chicago. What has always struck me as interesting is that we adults can fool ourselves into thinking whatever we wish. But children are not so easily fooled.

The fact that the children from Room 10 did not go to recess or lunch with the other kids emphasized their difference. Adults could pretend that they were part of the school. The kids knew better.

The shock of this separation made Eleanor feel as if she were on probation in the real school and living under a constant threat of being taken away from her friends.

This is also a story of how she discovered her disability. We had never hidden it from her but it took her this long to find it herself. To this day one of her favorite topics of conversation is Down syndrome and she greatly appreciates reassurance that she is loved for who she is and will not be "sent away" because of her disability.

Eleanor Helps Herself

Eleanor Bailey
Portland, Oregon

I am eleven years old and in fourth grade. This year some little girls came to my school. I heard some people say that they had Down syndrome. On a Saturday I asked my Mom, "Do I have Down syndrome?" Mom said that I do.

I went up to my bedroom and closed the door. I didn't cry but I shut the door and was mad and upset. I didn't want to have Down syndrome.

On Monday I went to school and I told my teacher, Mrs. Karr, that I had an announcement to make. She gave me the microphone and I said: "I have two things to say. First, I have Down syndrome and second, I am really scared that none of you will like me anymore."

My friends were really nice. They said they already knew that and that they still liked me. Some of them cried. I got lots of hugs.

But I am still not happy!

On Wednesday my Dad and I got on an airplane and went to Chicago. On the airplane I listened to my Walk Man. I have a song that goes "Clang, clang, rattle, bing, bang. I make my noise all day." I thought that is what I can do. Even with Down syndrome I can still make my noise.

We went to the TASH meeting. There were lots of really cool people there. We stayed in a big hotel. In our room there were two bathrooms. One had a shower and one had a bathtub. I made a sign that said "Girls" and put it on the door of the one with the bathtub. I didn't want my Dad to come in.

I took lots of baths. I thought if I took enough baths I could wash my Down syndrome away. I also thought I would put hairspray on it but my Mom and Dad won't let me have hairspray. I tried to put sunscreen on it because I thought that maybe then I wouldn't have to have it all the time. But my Dad said that none of that would work.

I have friends that were at TASH. My really special friend is Tia Nelis. She lives in Illinois. Tia has a disability but when Tia talk's people listen. They really listen. Tia is a leader and she really likes me. I told Tia that I have Down syndrome. I was surprised when she said that she had always known that. She said she didn't care. She said that I am an important person and that Down syndrome is not as important as being a wonderful person. When I grow up I want to be just like Tia.

I have other friends at TASH who told me the same thing. I meant a really nice person named Katie. Katie goes to college. Katie has Down syndrome. I also talked to my other friend Liz Obermayer. Liz has a new job and is moving to Maryland, which is a state. Liz has a disability but she is a leader too. She is on the Board of TASH. Liz goes to lots of meetings and people listen to her too.

I got my name from Eleanor Roosevelt. Lots of bad things happened in her life. I have read all about her. She was a leader. I also know about Rosa Parks, Martin Luther King, Nelson Mandela and Robert Kennedy. Lots of bad things happened to them but they were strong and were leaders. My Dad says they made people proud of whom they are and made them free.

I wish I didn't have Down syndrome, but I do and I am a person with lots of plans. When I wonder what to do I will remember my song. I will do what it says. I will go 'Clang, rattle, bing, bang and make my noise all day.' Even though I am sad I know I can be as tough as anyone. That is what I want to do.

Just be me.

Used with permission of *Mouth Magazine.*

Institution Closure

Oregon was one of the last states to close its huge institution for people with developmental disabilities. I had the privilege of being present on its last day of operation. (February, 2000)

I have included this article to remind us all that children who live and are educated in the community are relatively new phenomena.

Although segregation of people with disabilities is currently out of favor, it is our history, and one that can be repeated easily.

Farewell Fairview: You Will Not Be Missed

Michael T. Bailey

If only the 'inmates' of old could have benefited from today's more enlightened attitude.

In the end it was just green grass and vast, empty buildings. The mass of humanity going about its business; the smell, the bedlam, the shrieks, the love and the drama of human life are gone. In a moment all that became part of history; a part of our collective memory.

Last Thursday, a small group of staff, state officials and advocates met informally in front of LeBreton Hall on the grounds of the Fairview Training Center. Some stared into space, their minds occupied with memories, some joked, some dabbed at moist eyes, some took pictures. Over all of us lay the anticipation of a once-unimaginable and long awaited event. It happened, finally, at 1:15 p.m.

A green minivan pulled up in front of LeBreton and stopped. No one seemed to know what to do. A few of us waived to the occupant in the front passenger seat. He smiled and waived back. For him a new life was beginning as another, older and more ordered life came to an end.

The van pulled out and disappeared. Leaving in it was the last, the very last, resident of Fairview Training Center.

In the superintendent's office we examined the entries in the large, musky, leather-bound ledgers, their endless sheets filled with careful renderings, the pages yellow and stiff from age and from the dried ink so painstakingly applied by generations of clerks. On the pages are columns marked "inmates".

Here are the daily counts. "February 24, 1917, 371 inmates." Soon their number would exceed 3,000. The names of the new "inmates" were carefully recorded and each assigned an "inmate number". Also entries such as this: "March 16, 1921, inmate #...died. Remains shipped to family in Cave Junction." The ledgers are an archive not only of an institution but also of the meticulous detail attended to by the keepers of these "inmates."

There are scrapbooks of clippings from newspaper stories. Aging photos of goofy kids dressed up for a parade. Construction of the pond. Later, newsworthy pictures of young people bowling "in the community."

These are also stories of lost "inmates," of fires, murder and death. Images of faces smiling and laughing, a lasting testament to human spirit and resilience. I see that face every morning. My daughter has one just like it.

In 1981 the clippings began to tell another story; one of lawsuits, investigations, charges and counter-charges. That ended on Feb. 24, 2000 at 1:15 p.m. There will be no more clippings.

Slowly we walked around the silent and empty campus with two former "inmates" who remembered their lives at Fairview Training Center. The infirmary where one went for a knee operation only to learn that they had operated on her healthy hip by mistake. Another pointed out the spot where she was run over by a staff vehicle. To save money her knee was fused, rather than repaired. Thirty years later it still will not bend.

We walked into the empty "cottages," now smelling of cleaning products and echoing the sound of our footsteps. "Oh, no, it wasn't like this when I lived here," our commentator said. "Then there were no partitions of any kind. All of us girls slept on cots next to one another. There was never any privacy." She remembered how as a child she was frightened of "the big heads," the ones with hydrocephalus who leaned on the wall and groaned.

Finally, we passed the plaque on the wall of Fairview's first building. It commemorates the names of the superintendent, state officials and architect responsible for completing this project for the "Oregon Home for the Feeble Minded – 1919."

We walked back to LeBreton and got into the van. We drove off with one of the former "inmates." She had to return to her full-time job and at the end of the day would go home to her own apartment. There she would be alone with the memories of a life that once labeled her a "victim of…" and an "inmate" and now, finally, to that of a respected, financially independent and successful professional woman.

Farewell Fairview Training Center. You were born of a bad idea in 1908. You left us on a brisk and shining afternoon in the midst of an Oregon winter. Rest in Peace.

May your kind never pass our way again.

Table by State
School Year 2003-2004
Students on IEPs

State Abbreviation	Individual Educ. Program Students
AK	17,851
AL	122,698
AR	57,793
AZ	109,477
CA	680,831
CO	75,618
CT	69,829
DC	13,263
DE	17,171
FL	400,719
GA	186,342
HI	22,533
IA	63,886
ID	28,841
IL	316,733
IN	170,754
KS	65,092
KY	103,709
LA	101,288
MA	154,391

MD	108,141
ME	33,514
MI	244,610
MN	113,828
MO	144,752
MS	66,727
MT	19,267
NC	193,418
ND	13,774
NE	45,825
NH	29,390
NJ	223,144
NM	63,727
NV	45,201
NY*	Provided no data
OH	257,078
OK	93,047
OR	70,548
PA	253,129
RI	33,443
SC	109,561
SD	17,130
TN	171,594
TX	511,016
UT	57,745
VA	172,480
VT	14,737
WA	110,659
WI	127,129
WV	50,538
WY	13,430
TOTAL	**6,187,401**

(excluding NY)
In 1997 there were
347,126 students on IEPs
in New York.

APPENDIX

Web resources

RESOURCES FOR INCLUSION

Marsha Forest Foundation
http://www.inclusion.com/forestcentre.html

Beach Center on Disability, University of Kansas
http://www.beachcenter.org/

Parent Training and Information Centers
http://www.taalliance.org/centers/

Inclusion Resource Network
http://www.specialednet.com/inclusion.htm

Philosophy of Inclusion
http://www.uni.edu/coe/inclusion/

Assistive Technology for Inclusion
http://www.inclusive.co.uk/

The Nth Degree: Great gear, philosophy and ideas
http://www.thenthdegree.com/default.asp

LEGAL RESOURCES

Wrightslaw
http://www.wrightslaw.com/

Protection and Advocacy
http://www.napas.org/

NUTRITION AND WEB RESOURCES
http://www.disabilitysolutions.org/blog.htm

PARENT TRAINING CENTERS
http://www.taalliance.org/centers/

POSITIVE BEHAVIOR SUPPORTS

David Pitonyak
http://www.dimagine.com/

Mayer Shevin
http://www.shevin.org/

COMMUNITY LIVING FOR ADULTS

Marsha Katz
http://ruralinstitute.umt.edu/bios/katz.asp

Institute on Disability Culture, University of Hawaii
http://hometown.aol.com/sbrown8912/

QUESTIONS ABOUT MEDICAID AND SSI

Centers for Medicaid and Medicare Services
http://www.cms.hhs.gov/

Regulations on Title II Disability Benefits
http://www.google.com/search?hl=en&q=Title+II+Childhood+
Disability+Benefits&btnG=Google+Search

Supplemental Security Income
http://www.ssa.gov/disability/

What is SSI?
http://www.disabilitysecrets.com/question18.html

Medicaid Eligibility
http://www.cms.hhs.gov/MedicaidEligibility/

US Department of Education
http://www.ed.gov/index.jhtml

TRANSITION BENEFITS PLANNING

1.
SSA, www.ssa.gov

2.
Red Book on Employment Support, www.ssa.gov/redbook—
comments/suggestions, red.book.editor@ssa.gov

3.
Ticket To Work, www.ssa.gov/work or maxinc.com/ttw

4.
US Department of Education, www.usde.state.us
- Managing Your SSDI Benefits & Income Handbook
- Managing Your SSI Benefits & Income Handbook
- SSDI & SSI Benefit Programs & Work Incentives—Produced by Michael Walling, service Enhancement Associates at www.wallinginc.com

5.
Institute for Child Health Policy, www.ichp.edu

6.
School to Work Learning & Information Center, www.stw.ed.gov

7.
Academy for Educational Development, www.aed.org

8.
National Youth Leadership Network, www.nyln.org

9.
Special Education News, www.specialednews.com

10.
Federal Maternal & Child Health Bureau, www.mchbhrtw.org

11.
RRTC on Workplace Supports, www.worksupport.com

Printed in the United States
47860LVS00005B/255

9 781424 127955